THE DRAMA OF
OPERA

To Nicholas and Jonathan
With my love

THE DRAMA OF

OPERA

Exotic and Irrational Entertainment

MYER FREDMAN

With a Foreword by Dame Joan Sutherland and Maestro Richard Bonynge

sussex
ACADEMIC
PRESS

BRIGHTON • PORTLAND

2 4 6 8 10 9 7 5 3 1

First published 2003 in Great Britain by
SUSSEX ACADEMIC PRESS
PO Box 2950
Brighton BN2 5SP

and in the United States of America by
SUSSEX ACADEMIC PRESS
920 NE 58th Ave   Suite 300
Portland, Oregon 97213-3786

British Library Cataloguing in Publication Data
A CIP catalogue record for this book is available from the British Library.

Library of Congress Cataloging-in-Publication Data has been applied for.
Fredman, Myer.
The drama of opera : exotic and irrational entertainment / Myer
Fredman ; with a foreword by Dame Joan Sutherland and Richard Bonynge.
p. cm.
Includes bibliographical references (p.   ) and index.
ISBN 1–903900–49 2 (alk. paper) —
ISBN 1–903900–50–6 (pbk. : alk. paper)
I. Opera. I. Sutherland, Joan, 1926– II. Bonynge, Richard. III. Title.
ML1700.F72 2003
782.1—dc21
                                              2003004321

Typeset and designed by G&G Editorial, Brighton
Printed and bound in the UK by The Cromwell Press, Trowbridge, Wiltshire
This book is printed on acid-free paper.

Contents

'An exotic and irrational entertainment'

Opera – Exotic . . . Irrational . . . Entertainment . . .

The Creators

The Re-Creators

Contents

Study and Beyond

The Complete Rehearsal Period

Contents

The Administration

The Audience

Interlude: Operatic Mishaps and Other Cautionary Tales

Opera Companies

Past, Present and Future?

Foreword

This fascinating book is for those who love opera, those who know nothing about opera and especially for those who know what they like but don't know why. Every piece of information you could conceivably want to know about the 'exotic and irrational entertainment' is to be found between these covers.

Myer Fredman has passed a lifetime of experience in the opera house and writes with understanding and humour to produce a valuable insight into an extraordinary world. Whether you think you know it all or if you know nothing, read on to discover a myriad of fascinating insights into this curious genre of entertainment.

Although a book about opera, it is all sound common sense — a quality not always in evidence in the hallowed halls of the opera house. The book is the opposite of stuffy . . . full of bon mots, stories and opinions (strange as some of them may be) of many musicians and composers who do not always think as one might expect. There is good advice for professionals and great help for the laity - given with understated humour.

Read about the backstage, the preparation, the sets, costumes, producers, conductors, singers — and their foibles with both sides of the coin presented. We read of producers who 'regurgitate platitudes based on little or no experience' but also of the sensitive producer who can create the environment needed for the music.

We read of Beethoven's notorious unvocal writing in *Fidelio*, of how a contemporary critic wrote that Mozart was a noisy, dissonant composer with no talent for writing for the voice.

Berlioz said 'I loathe Divas' and Debussy thought dogs more entertaining than great prima donnas.

Some composers had scant respect for the opera – Delius thought ninety minutes to two hours long enough for any opera. He also thought (even in 1927) that the average man was accustomed to having his mind made up by advertisements – as is still apparent today with the power of money and the press.

Verdi, when asked for some specific themes about opera opined only that 'the theatre should be full'.

Debussy thought that the Paris Opera looked like a railway station on the outside and a Turkish bath on the inside – what might he have thought of the present-day Bastille?

Wagner with his virulent anti-Semitism affected Hitler to the extent that the Nazi myth of racial purity grew out of Wagner's theories.

You will no doubt be intrigued to read that Dame Ethel Smyth (composer of 'The Wreckers') occasionally conducted with a toothbrush.

While modern opera productions are becoming more bizarre and show scant respect for their original creators, it is amusing to realize that *plus ça change, plus c'est la même chose.* A 19th century production of Mozart's *Don Giovanni* brought the body of Donna Anna on stage at the end of the piece while the chorus of mourners sang the *Dies Irae* from his (not yet written) Requiem.

Foreword by Dame Joan Sutherland and Richard Bonynge

The singers are both helpfully advised and excoriated at the same time. I wonder who was the singer who delivered the word 'Abscheulicher' with such vehemence that her dentures flew out and she spent the whole of the aria groping around the stage looking for them.

Myer Fredman warns that ambition is vital to a successful career but when excessive can lead to disaster. He is caustic about singers who present themselves at auditions (and rehearsals?) in a dishevelled state as if they had slept on a park bench overnight.

He warns talented singers who begin too soon that their careers may be over before they have really begun. 'However difficult it may be to open a door of opportunity it is even more so to arrive unless the talent is on a par with the ambition'. Singers' temperament is frequently a synonym for bad manners or uncontrolled nerves, horrible results ensuing.

Despite the warnings we realize that this is a book written by someone who loves and has lived opera, that combination of all the arts, so utterly fulfilling or completely infuriating.

The human voice at its best is the greatest of all musical instruments and it is music that elevates opera above all other theatre.

Every facet of this irrational art form with its curious conventions is discussed entertainingly by Myer Fredman – his love of Mozart and Britten shines through the pages. The book concludes with a splendid glossary of musical and theatrical terms and an index.

Les Avants, Switzerland
Dame Joan Sutherland and Richard Bonynge
August 2003

‖: x :‖

Preface and Acknowledgements

The Drama of Opera sets out to describe the drama that takes place within the world of opera rather than focusing on individual operatic plots, which are well documented elsewhere. Like all other art forms, opera has often suffered from the so-called 'philistines'; indeed, its very purpose has been subject to mis-information, ignorance and inverted snobbery. Yet like the phoenix, opera has always risen from the ashes with renewed vigour to captivate each new generation with changes for the better in some respects and for the worse in others.

This survey of the drama within the world of opera over the past four hundred years provides some indication of how opera, and its acceptance by the public, may progress in the future as our rapidly changing Western world succumbs to more and more technological means of communication. What is vitally critical, and especially so from the conductor's perspective, is that current musical standards are maintained and promoted. Likewise, the opera-going public has to be engaged with an even greater degree of informed understanding (including constructive criticism), whether high art or simply pure entertainment. Opera needs to be met halfway by a musically advantaged public through education – in the proper sense of the word – without any patronizing bombast.

The theme of *'exotic entertainment'* allows for the exploration of every aspect of opera's creation and re-creation, and much that follows is the result of the author's experience at all levels of musical expertise from Repetiteur, Chorus Master to Musical Director as well as the Head of an Opera School. The aim of this book therefore is to place readers within the drama of opera in order that they may gain a greater recognition of the complexity of staging opera and an insight into the everyday dramas in which all those involved participate before all their efforts unite in performance.

There have been a number of attempts to compose an opera about *The Drama of Opera* but only two have really succeeded, both with music by Richard Strauss. His last opera, *Capriccio*, took as its basic plot the insoluble conundrum of which is more important in opera — the words or the music. His earlier *Ariadne auf Naxos* took as its starting point many aspects of opera with which this book is concerned. In its Vorspiel (Prelude), the characters are a composer (a mezzo-soprano travesty *rôle* like Cherubino modeled perhaps on Mozart), a Heldentenor, a Prima Donna, a Dancing Master, a Perruquier and *commedia dell'arte* figures; the text even refers to the expense involved in staging an opera. The second act is a complete opera in itself fusing *opera seria*, based on a mythological subject, with *opera buffa*, based on the *commedia dell'arte* archetypes. During the Vorspiel's closing pages, Strauss and his librettist, Hofmannsthal, put into the mouth of their composer an imperishable text that any performer, or lover of music and opera, should always keep in mind: *'Was ist denn Musik?'* (What then is Music?). He then answers himself: *'Musik ist eine heilige Kunst'* (Music is a noble Art) — *heilige* (noble) being the operative word. The essence of that question and answer were at the back of my mind as the final section of this book was being considered and written. *What do the past and present have in store for the future? Will opera and so-called classical music retain its 'nobility'?* I sincerely hope so. And if my experience with young, aspiring performers and enthusiastic groups of opera lovers are anything to go by, I am reassured that opera will continue to provide a valuable contribution to art and society.

The plate section pictures are courtesy of Mike Hoban, resident photographer at Glyndebourne. The Papageno print is courtesy of Bibliothèque nationale de France.

I thank Ms. Jenifer Eddy, the Director of Jenifer Eddy Artists Management, for her invaluable insight as both a one-time artist in her own right, and more recently as an Artist's Manager. I also wish to thank the Adelaide Centre for Physical Fitness for its report on the cardiovascular conditions involved in the physical and spiritual act of conducting. Last but by no means least, I thank my wife for her painstaking work in checking the book as it developed from initial idea through to the script, and finally to its publication.

Myer Fredman
Tasmania, August 2003

'An exotic and irrational entertainment'

Dr. Samuel Johnson (1709–84) has been regularly quoted as stating that opera is *'an exotic and irrational entertainment'* but the complete quotation from his *Lives of the English Poets* reads quite differently: *'an exotic and irrational entertainment which has always been combated, and always has prevailed'*. The complete sentence acknowledges that, for the worthy doctor, opera was a viable adjunct to leisure and well able to survive the 'slings and arrows of outrageous misfortune'. It does remain unclear, however, as to whether or not his first five words referred to Italian opera being sung in the original language in England or opera in general, but nevertheless the mis-quotation has been used ever since by those who criticize opera, to damning affect. It is worth defining Dr. Johnson's exact words:

Opera . . . *'Work, action, performance, doing, institution or office of works'*. The Italian word, opera, originally had no connection at all with music but it has come to mean the fusion of music and text in a dramatic setting, while an opera company certainly qualifies as *an institution or office of works!* The designation 'Opera' was actually noted by the English diarist John Evelyn in 1644 during a visit to Italy, although such *entertainments* were usually headed with the title *melodramma* or *dramma per musica*, while in France they were headed *Tragèdie Lyrique*.

In his *La Dictionnaire de la Musique* (1764) the poet, philosopher and musician Jean-Jacques Rousseau wrote that *'the constituent parts of an opera are the poem; the music and the decorative production. Through poetry one speaks to the mind, through music to the ear, through painting to the eyes, and the whole unites to move the heart and to produce the same impression through these various organs.'* Oratorio fulfils one of these requisites, being a setting of a text, but it is intended for concert performance without dramatic movement, and more often than not, on a religious subject. Chinese Opera cannot be

‖: I :‖

considered as opera in the Western sense of the word because apart from singing and dancing, it involves other virtuoso skills such as juggling and acrobatics that would be way beyond the expertise of most Italian Divas and German Helden Tenors!

Opera should never be considered as simply a play with music; conversely, a libretto devoid of its musical setting could never grace the stage as a straight play. Brilliant as Da Ponte's libretto is for *Così fan tutte*, it would never succeed as a spoken drama and similarly *La bohème*. There are exceptions, of course, like Maeterlinck's *Pelleas & Melisande*, Dürrenmatt's *Der besuch der alten Dame* and, although never attempted, Hoffmannsthal's *Der Rosenkavalier*. The text of a libretto shorn of its music is often as banal as a modern 'soap opera', yet the greatest composers are able to transport the audience into another world – the world of the imagination and the spirit – with the plot unfolding and its dramatic timing all stemming from the music. Logically it must be the persuasive power of music that differentiates opera from what is usually referred to as 'straight' theatre.

Like every other entertainment, opera has certain well-defined conventions; the first is that the drama is sung rather than spoken more often than not, and the action is suspended sometimes to allow the music time to speak directly from *'the heart to the heart'* as Beethoven believed. Another convention permits a word's elongation over a much longer period of time than is vocally or histrionically possible in the theatre; a third, is that words and even whole sentences are repeated for musical balance, emotional emphasis, or for different inflexions which an imaginative artist will seize upon. In eighteenth- and nineteenth-century operas this often led to farewells taking far longer than in real life yet the endless setting of *addio* or *lebewohl* is able to persuade the audience to overlook any irrationality.

Yet another operatic convention is the overture. In the straight theatre the curtain rises and the play begins immediately; whereas in

‖: 2 :‖

opera this does not occur until after the overture has concluded. The overture usually sets the atmosphere and helps to quieten the audience (hopefully) or allow for latecomers. Verdi ignored that tradition for *Otello* and *Falstaff* and Puccini always plunged straight into the drama, which seems to have become the convention ever since with, possibly, a few exceptions. For similar dramatic effect, he indicated at the start of Act 2 in *La bohème* the exact point where the curtain should rise some time **after** the chorus begins to sing – but this *coup de théâtre* is now considered *passé* – and very few producers comply with Puccini's express wish.

In 1690, the poet, John Dryden wrote a splendid dedication for Purcell to present to the Duke of Somerset which conveys the equality of music and poetry in opera: *'Musik and Poetry, have been acknowledg'd Sisters, which walking hand in hand, support each other; as Poetry is the harmony of Words, so Musick is that of Notes, and as Poetry is a Rise above Prose and Oratory, so is Musick the exaltation of Poetry. Both of them may excel apart, but sure they are most excellent when they are joyn'd, because nothing is then wanting to either of their Perfections; for thus they appear like Wit and Beauty in the same Person.'*

Singers in that era took such great liberties with words and music that by the time Gluck arrived on the scene he had to instigate drastic reforms, as mentioned in his Preface to *Alceste* in 1767: *'I have thought it necessary to reduce music to its true function, which is that of seconding poetry in the expression of sentiments and dramatic situations of a story, neither interrupting the action nor detracting from its vividness by useless and superfluous ornament.'* Despite its wording, Gluck was not actually arguing for the supremacy of text over music but against singers' excesses. Some years later Mozart was more unequivocal in a letter to his father: *'In opera the text must be the obedient daughter of the music.'*

There has always been considerable controversy as to which is the more important in opera – the text or the music. Indeed, Salieri (1750–1825) actually composed a one-act opera on this very subject with the title of *Prima la musica e poi le parole* (First the music and then the words). It was first performed in 1786 as part of a double-bill with *Der Schauspieldirektor* by Mozart who, legend has it, was later poisoned by Salieri. Their fictitious rivalry was also to become the subject of an opera (*Mozart & Salieri*) by Rimsky-Korsakov. As recently as 1942, Richard Strauss used Salieri's title as the basis for his last opera, *Capriccio*.

Exotic . . . has a number of dictionary definitions including *'strikingly unusual or colourful in appearance'*, and the majority of operas can certainly be categorized as such. Verdi did not hesitate to compose an *exotic* and *irrational* full-blown women's chorus for the three witches in his *Macbeth* based on Shakespeare's tragedy. Bizet was captivated by the exoticism of the gypsy, Carmen and her associates; Puccini's *La fanciulla del West* is a cowboy opera and his *Turandot* is set in the forbidden city of Peking/Beijing; while Donizetti's *Amelia di Liverpool* takes place in the mountains around the English city where there are none. Auber's *La muette de Portici* not only has a heroine who is literally dumb – a Prima Donna in all but voice – but she commits suicide by leaping from the balcony of the Royal Palace into the mouth of Vesuvius which is nearly ten miles away. More recently, a German composer wrote an opera about Scott of the Antarctic in which the chorus were penguins! Wolf-Ferrari's delicious *Il Segreto di Susanna* exposes the secret vice of a wife (her cigarette smoking) and Richard Strauss's *Intermezzo* when it first appeared was highly exotic, even bizarre, for the composer's own household was blatantly recreated on stage.

Irrational . . . the dictionary definition is *'without the faculty of, or not endowed with reason'*, which Bertolt Brecht expanded in his notes about his collaboration with Kurt Weill on *Aufstieg und Fall der Stadt Mahagonny*, written just after the First World War. *The irrationality of opera lies in the fact that rational elements are employed, solid reality is aimed at, but at the same time it is all washed out by the music. A dying man is real.*' Brecht may have argued strongly against the irrationality of opera but even Shakespeare was irrational for putting blank verse and poetry into the mouths of his characters, yet the Bard is accepted without question. In ballet, not a word is spoken while the sixteenth and seventeenth-century painters dressed their biblical figures in contemporary clothes, with decidedly European features! Mozart is similarly irrational in that in *Don Giovanni*, the Commendatore's statue moves and speaks (sings), and in *Le nozze di Figaro*, Cherubino sings with a female voice although seemingly a boy. It must therefore be noted that irrationality has never been a hindrance for the creative artist.

Arguably the most *irrational* opera house ever built was Glyndebourne, which opened its doors in 1934. Nestling in the folds of the Sussex Downs far from 'the madding crowd', the audience has to travel from the metropolis by one means or another (sometimes by helicopter) for an early evening performance with a long interval for dinner or a picnic. Glydnebourne's very first programme included these pithy items by its founder, John Christie: *Mozart was born on January 27th. 1756, in Salzburg. Visited London in 1764 (aged 8). Händel died in 1759. Mozart also visited Tunbridge Wells.*' John Christie's programme notes also contained a description of the new theatre's acoustics: *This Festival Opera House has been built by the Ringmer Motor Works, who have in conjunction with their architectural and acoustics advisers, undertaken to build a building where the **acoustics** are satisfactory. They have succeeded in producing a building where the acoustics are supremely good. Every whisper on the stage can be heard all over the auditorium. The singers have never found any building so good to sing in. This work is of National Importance. The results are not accidental. At first the results were good; then, as the work progressed further, very good; then when the chairs were installed, as bad as they could be; and now the acoustics have been corrected (at a cost of a few pounds), so that, at last, they are marvelously good. The result has not been accidental, but is the result of the application of Science, of elementary Physics,* *and chiefly commonsense. The balance of sound in the front row is almost perfect. This is accidental but "it never rains but it pours".'*

Entertainment . . . *'Something affording diversion or amusement'* well described opera in the time of Dr. Johnson but it has come to mean any drama, melodrama, romance, tragedy, the supernatural, sport or virtually any subject that will attract the paying public. During and after the Renaissance, the wealthy Italian families and the aristocracy encouraged the performance of music in their palaces, so it was a logical step to involve music in their dramatic entertainments. Such presentations took place within the family apartments; theatres only came into existence with the rise of the merchant class (the bourgeoisie), perhaps to emulate the aristocracy. The theatres could accommodate larger audiences so more people were able to enjoy what was soon to become known as opera but as yet there were no orchestra pits or darkened auditoriums. These only evolved during the nineteenth century when even larger theatres were built, creating the need for larger orchestras, and candle illumination gave way to lighting by gas, and later, electricity.

Concert-going began to equate with opera as the preferred entertainment for the middle and higher socio-economic groups, and intellectual snobbery started to foster the idea that opera was a somewhat inferior form of music. Even the Italian masters of melody (and the orchestra) like Verdi and later, Puccini, were scorned because of the overpowering German symphonic influence perpetrated by the new race of autocratic conductors who were avid disciples of Wagner. The designation *entertainment* was usurped by a more lofty title, 'Art', which previously had only referred to painting. It was now to be elevated to 'High Art', as epitomized by Wagner's quasi-religious rituals.

*T*he Creators
*C*omposers and the Language of Music

The meaning of music cannot be adequately explained, as it is highly subjective, yet music is as precise a language as that involving words which are built from vowels and consonants. Likewise, music consists of pitch and rhythm that together form phrases. Composers who write for the voice are able to express themselves in words and music *simultaneously!* Stravinsky, however, was firmly convinced that music did not mean anything at all whereas Richard Strauss maintained that he could even portray a teaspoon in music, as in his *Symphony Domestica!* Others believe that music reaches into the deepest subconscious of the soul, so the essence of music must always remain a subjective mystery.

In opera, the language of music heightens the meaning of the text with, for instance, the shape and colour of a highly evocative cello or horn phrase, which can suggest a variety of different moods and emotions. Other instances are the bare, open fifths when the third act of *La bohème* opens which conjure up the bitter cold of an early morning in winter at the gates of Paris; the trombones reflect the supernatural and solemn moments in *Don Giovanni* and *Die Zauberflöte*; and the strings mirror the pitter patter of a lover's beating heart in *Così fan tutte*. In a letter to his father when composing *Die Entführung aus dem Serail*, Mozart clearly stated what music could do, at least for him, '*You can feel the trembling, the faltering, and even see how his throbbing breast begins to swell; I have expressed this by a crescendo.*'

It has often been said that the very first music is the soft, cooing sounds as a newborn baby suckles at its mother's breast, though more guttural sounds must have developed as primeval tribes discovered that such sounds helped them to move heavy boulders and dead carcasses into their caves. Similarly the early fishermen found that by chanting in rhythm, they rowed their dugouts and canoes much better, and with less effort. Gradually these elements of melody and rhythm coalesced into music. The earliest known documentation is the Bible when the Children of Israel prayed to their one God, King David recited (or sang) his Psalms and Joshua exhorted his trumpeters at Jericho (although this has now been exposed as something of a myth). *Mousikē*, the ancient Greek word, defined all the arts that were inspired by the Muses but gradually it came to mean only the art of music. It was used extensively in the theatres and for civic and religious ceremonies, but it had neither harmony nor accompaniment; yet it did have a kinship with mathematics, as mentioned in the writings of Pythagoras and Plato. Little is known about Greek music but it was essentially improvised and used the melodic rise and fall of the spoken language punctuated by its verbal rhythm. The Thespians – actors and singers – were such virtuoso exhibitionists that Plutarch referred to their chanting (singing) as mere sound without any substance – an observation that was to be voiced many times in the centuries that followed.

In medieval times it was believed that music was derived from the Greek conception of mathematics and the movement of the spheres, yet the foremost universal power was, incredibly, inaudible to mankind. The philosopher Boethius was convinced that the highest form of music existed in both the body and the soul in perfect harmony as *musica mundana* and *musica humana* while vocal and instrumental music, *musica instrumentalis*, was at a lower level. Augustine extended this idea further in that music had the ability to purify the soul and that there was a connection between music and the emotions; rhythm and melody were allied to *corporal* (physical) numbers heard by the ear while the soul experienced *eternal* (spiritual) numbers. Both Boethius and Augustine may have been unconsciously influenced by the contrasting powers of Apollo and Dionysus, which are still relevant today, while *musica munda*, *musica humana* and *corporal* versus *eternal* foreshadowed today's dichotomy between *classical* and *popular* music. Their insights into the meaning of music will be examined in greater detail later.

Writing an opera has never been merely a matter of composers using words as clothes pegs on which to hang their beautiful melodies. The greatest have always found that a comparable rise and fall in the vocal line could complement the rise and fall in the emotions and thoughts of an operatic character. Monteverdi (1567–1643) was one of the first to fuse music and text into an indivisible entity, and, in the spirit of the Renaissance, he rediscovered how Homer recited his great epics while accompanying himself on the lyre (hence the word, lyrical). Monteverdi replaced the lyre with various contemporary stringed instruments, as is well documented, but contemporary vocal technique can only be surmised. One thing for sure is that the art of singing must have been quite different to the *Bel Canto* technique of two centuries later, the reason being that the halls and salons in the palaces did not need the vocal projection that had to be developed for the larger theatres in the nineteenth century. Voice production during Monteverdi's time was probably equivalent to the sound of his stringed instruments, i.e. soft-grained and with little volume – like that of our very young singers today. Monteverdi's use of brass instruments, on the other hand, as, for example, the trumpet parts in his Vespers of 1610, show that for certain spectacular occasions demanding greater brilliance, a more robust sound was equally possible.

In a letter of that year, Monteverdi wrote, '*I have noticed that the interlocutore are winds, Cupids, little Zephyrs and Sirens; consequently many sopra-*

nos will be needed, and it can also be stated that the winds have to sing — that is, the *Zephyrs and Boreals. How, dear Sir, can I imitate the speech of the winds if they do not speak? And how can I, by such means, move the passions? . . . Music can suggest, without any words, the noise of winds, and the bleating of sheep, the neighing of horses and so on and so forth; but it cannot imitate the speech of winds because no such things exist.'*

The language of music was greatly advanced by Mozart's intuitive selection of keys with which to reflect a character's emotions. In particular, the key of G minor had a special place in his tonal palette, as in Ilia's first aria in *Idomeneo* and Pamina's in *Die Zauberflöte* (and in countless other works). Similarly, F major represented a character's earthy quality while F minor was reserved for parody; A major infused his most romantic and sensual duets and D major, the aristocracy (usually with trumpets and drums). For further information about Mozart's use of keys, see the author's *From Idomeneo to Die Zauberflöte*, which explores the subject in greater detail. A key's emotional colour has always inspired different responses from different composers. For instance, in 1754 the composer and harpsichordist Rameau wrote, '*One cites the sharp as a sign of strength and joy for one raises the voice in the same manner in anger etc. and the flat as a sign of softness and weakness, etc. as when one lowers the voice in the same way.*' Similarly Jean-Jacques Rousseau, who was both a composer and philosopher (not necessarily incompatible), wrote, '*Good composers prefer D major for bright songs, C minor for pathetic expression, and F minor for sombre or lugubrious moments.*'

It is well known that melody, harmony and rhythm are the basis of all Western music but without phrasing and tempo, music remains inanimate and arid. Monteverdi noted that '*All the best philosophers declare that a Pyrrhic, that is to say, a rapid tempo should be used for all war-like or agitated dances, and on the contrary a slow tempo for the opposite situations*'. During the baroque period there were two basic tempos, fast and slow, derived from the human heart-rate of approximately eighty pulses to the minute; each had two sub-divisions – moderately fast/very fast; moderately slow/very slow – and if there were no tempo indications, then the smallest rhythmic cell would be a sufficient guide. Then as orchestras grew larger and the conductor – rather than the first violinist – took command, tempo indications and their qualification such as *assai* and *con brio* began to dominate as the heart/pulse-rate became redundant. The metronome was invented during Beethoven's lifetime and it also became an arbiter of tempo. But its relentless tick-tock has proved to be a hindrance rather than a help ever since because a phrase has to breathe to create an ebb and flow if it is to be musical.

From even before the baroque period, the score was considered more like a blueprint than today and was performed with whatever instruments were at hand. When three hundred years later baroque opera became relevant once again, Raymond Leppard 'realized' Monteverdi's *L'incoronazione di Poppea* incorporating the continuo instruments of the era with the strings of today. In the 1960s, the old instrument revival had not yet begun and though Leppard added two viola lines to the string parts, his harmonic structure was still built on the original bass line. After the revelation of Monteverdi's incredible originality, Leppard was accused of creating too lush a sound. More recently, Hans Werner Henze's free adaptation of Monteverdi's *Il ritorno d'Ulisse in patria* – using the resources of the modern orchestra – was similarly attacked. Despite the critical purists who insist that baroque music must only be played as it is documented, neither Leppard nor Henze had taken any undue liberty. For them, as for baroque musicians, Monteverdi's original had been a blueprint rather than an exact working score, as performers from the nineteenth century on would have expected.

There were three basic styles during the sixteenth and seventeenth centuries – Italian, French and English, with J. S. Bach composing keyboard suites in all three. Such suites grew out of the aristocratic *entertainments* and were usually inspired by the rhythm and phrase lengths of dances like the Pavan (Pavane or Pavin), Galliard, Courante, Allemande, Gigue, Bourée, and the later Gavotte and Menuet (Menuetto or Minuet). Only the Menuet survived in the eighteenth century in the symphonies of Haydn and Mozart but that dance also disappeared when it was transfigured by Beethoven into the faster Scherzo.

During the eighteenth century it was the accepted practice for composers to provide arias or ensembles for another's opera so that many of Mozart's Concert Arias are actually leftovers from other composers' works that are now forgotten; the reverse favour does not seem to have been granted – maybe because his lesser talented rivals knew they could not hope to compete with his genius. Such a forgotten opera was the recently discovered *Der Stein der Weisen* (The Philosopher's Stone), which was composed by a 'committee' of five that included Mozart who contributed a number of arias and ensembles. One of the other four was Emanuel Schikaneder who commissioned Mozart to write *Die Zauberflöte* the following year, in which the other three took part, one of whom sang Tamino and played the flute on stage. Mozart was also not averse to composing alternative arias for some singers to suit their vocal accomplishments as the Prague and Vienna editions of *Don Giovanni* indicate. Unfortunately the substitutions have created problems ever since in that a tenor may be able to sing Ottavio's *Dalla sua pace* very well but be vocally uncomfortable in *Il mio tesoro*. Similarly in *Le nozze di Figaro*, Susanna usually sings *Venite, inginochiatevi* but three years after its première, Mozart composed *Un moto di gioia* for Adriana Faresi, which is not nearly so pertinent to her dressing Cherubino as a girl despite the latter aria's considerable charm. Even more of a problem is when a soprano insists on singing *Al desio di chi t'adora* instead of *Deh vieni non tarda* in Act 4. The former is overlong and it comes near the end of a tiring evening for Susanna who is hardly ever off the stage; its coloratura is not within the capabilities of most lyric sopranos, and to make matters worse, Mozart's scoring includes basset horns which do not play elsewhere in the opera so their inclusion is inordinately expensive.

No composer could even begin to write an opera without having received the libretto, but from time to time there have been exceptional circumstances. Mozart composed the Trio that concludes Act I of *Die Entführung aus dem Serail* before he received the text, having informed his librettist (Gottlieb Stephanie) what the rhythm and scansion had to be to fit the music he had already put on paper. Puccini was also not averse to composing an aria before the text had arrived on his desk; Musetta's Waltz, 'Quando me'n vo' in Act 2 of *La bohème* had originally been a piano piece which he then scored for brass band to launch a battleship before it finally found its way into the scene at the Café Momus. Puccini certainly did not believe in wasting a good tune!

Some composers have taken it upon themselves to tamper with another's work. Mahler edited Weber's *Die drei Pintos* and Rimsky-Korsakov 'improved' Mussorgsky's *Boris Godunov*, but the most blatant would have to be Wagner's incursion into Mozart's *Don Giovanni*, which he re-orchestrated in places and inserted a recitative which he himself composed. Some have a feeling for a dramatic text yet are incapable of writing a viable opera despite various attempts. Haydn, Schubert, Schumann, Mendelssohn, Brahms and Fauré were all in this category and, although they were able to set romantic, mysterious, comic and tragic texts as their songs amply indicate, they lacked a sense of theatre in their musical language to paint on the larger canvas of opera. The most operatically *irrational* composer must surely have been Mahler – a great conductor in both opera as Artistic Director of the Vienna State Opera and on the concert platform – yet he never composed a single opera. Even so, his nine (or ten) symphonies are highly dramatic and sometimes even over-theatrical but their occasional echoes of opera probably stemmed from his regular working life as a conductor.

Beethoven only composed one opera. *Fidelio* was premièred in 1805 but it ran for only three performances as the audience consisted largely of French army officers because Napoleon had entered Vienna only a few days previously and the Viennese were frightened to venture out of doors. As with so much of his music, Beethoven had to wrestle with his material before he was completely satisfied so *Fidelio* only reached its final form after nine years of trial and error. Its first version had the title *Leonore* and some of the arias and ensembles were considerably longer, with the last scene taking place in the dungeon rather than outside the prison walls. Beethoven was also dissatisfied with his first *Leonore* Overture and had two more attempts before arriving at what is now the Overture to *Fidelio* with music that bears no relation to the other three. The current overture is a more appropriate start to the first scene which was in the style of a *singspiel* before the Quartet took the atmosphere of the opera into another world.

By the beginning of the nineteenth century music had started to reflect the emerging nationalism in Europe so that the music of Weber and his German colleagues was markedly different to that of their Italian contemporaries. Opera was now categorized as 'Art' as much as *entertainment* and Romantic artists were to add another dimension to the language of music. Composers began to explore the dramatic possibilities of their inherited chromatic (coloured) progressions from Mozart's *Don Giovanni* and his other excursions into the harmonic underworld. By the middle of the century, and Wagner's supremacy over all other European music, composers reacted by searching for a new musical language and discovered the abundant folk music of their native countries. The *exotic* Slavonic idiom came into the orbit of such composers as Dvořák, Smetana, and further east, the Russians were headed by Cui and Glinka. But Verdi, the patriotic Italian, avoided the trend even in his very English *Falstaff* – perhaps because England was still to discover its own folk music! Verdi was, first and foremost, an opera composer (apart from his very operatic Requiem, a string quartet and a handful of choral works) and he did not hesitate in chiding the young Puccini for being too symphonic: *'Our music differs from German music. Their symphonies can live in halls; their chamber music can live in the home. Our music, I say, resides principally in the theatre but the theatres can no longer exist without government subsidy.'* Verdi was probably referring to Puccini's 'symphonic' scores like *Crisantemi, Preludio, Capriccio Sinfonico* and the *Messa di Gloria*, but the younger composer went on to meld his southern Italian melodic instinct with the northern European symphonic style having carefully studied the orchestral techniques of Wagner, Debussy and other contemporaries. The opening of Act 2 in *La bohème* has a family likeness to Stravinsky's *Petrushka* (unmistakably Russian) and is thus a splendid example of two seemingly incompatible composers ostensibly using the same musical language!

Whilst composing *Turandot* Puccini wrote, *'I have the great weakness of being able to write only when my puppet executioners are moving on the scene. If only I could be a purely symphonic writer! I should then at least cheat time — and my public. But that was not for me. I was born so many years ago — oh, so many, too many, almost a century — and Almighty God touched me with His little finger and said "Write for the theatre — mind only for the theatre". And I have obeyed the supreme command.'* It was as if Verdi's ghost was standing behind him as he wrote those lines. Puccini was not only a complete man of the theatre but an astute businessman as well, for the time span of virtually all his arias were comparable with one side of the recently invented gramophone record (wax) that were becoming highly profitable!

Composers have always found inspiration in the universal myths of humanity — especially those concerned with adultery, faith and salvation as exemplified by Don Juan, the Abraham and Isaac parable, and the quest for God and/or the eternal feminine. Mozart was not the only composer to have set the Don Juan myth. In fact *Don Giovanni* espouses two mythological subjects, the profligate and the blasphemer, a variation of the Don Juan legend and concerned indirectly with the subject of everlasting youth, hence the legend of Faust. The second myth – faith – stems from the Biblical story of Abraham preparing to sacrifice his son to his God – which also occurs in Gluck's *Iphigénie en Aulide*, *Iphigénie en Tauride* and *Alceste*; although arguably the greatest interpretation of this myth about self-sacrifice is Mozart's *Idomeneo*. The third myth – the quest – inspired many composers to set the legend of Orpheus and his descent into Hades to rescue Euridice. Other quests include *Die Zauberflöte*, *Fidelio*, *Der Fliegende Holländer* and more recently *The Midsummer Marriage*, all of which embody the search for truth, the meaning of life in both its spiritual and corporeal sense (harking back to the music of the spheres), and the everlasting search for the feminine ideal.

The path a composer has to follow from the initial desire to write an opera to its realization in performance is usually very arduous. Finding the right subject can easily take many years and then the chosen librettist may be uninterested in the subject matter so the search has to begin all over again. If all is well, however, a period of gestation for both the composer and the librettist commences but even then the project may flounder at any time due to waning enthusiasm. If their work does reach a satisfactory conclusion, there still remains the problem for an unknown composer of promoting their offspring unless there is a patron or an opera company in the offing.

A salutary example occurred when Benjamin Britten returned to England from America in 1945 as a relatively unknown composer.

Joan Cross, the manager of Sadlers Wells during the Second World War, wholeheartedly believed in Britten's operatic genius but she had to persuade her very reluctant company to consider his opera for performance. Joan Cross overruled all opposition, *Peter Grimes* was produced and the rest is operatic history. Having learnt from the experience, Britten created the English Opera Group for which he composed *The Rape of Lucretia, Albert Herring, The Turn of the Screw, Lets make an Opera,* and his realizations of Purcell's *Dido & Aeneas* and Gay's *The Beggar's Opera.*

Very few composers are prepared to write an opera without a commission of some sort because of the enormous labour, time and finance involved; usually other creative work has to be put aside. If under contract to a publisher, especially if an international organization, the enormous expense of commissioning a vocal score has to be arranged and the copying of orchestral parts well looked after. Yet, even so, the cost of a new opera can be a stumbling block for any opera company when considering future repertoire. There is no guarantee that it will turn out to be a success with both the critics and the public, and a successful première may still not warrant a revival for any number of reasons.

Opera has always had a high mortality rate as the annals of opera abundantly indicate. Every year, many are composed but only a few survive and, paradoxically, the most popular – *La traviata, Carmen,* and *Madama Butterfly* among them – had disastrous premières and only later were they to become the mainstay of companies that now could not survive without them. It is sometimes forgotten that virtually every operatic composer undergoes a period of trial and error before arriving at maturity and only on rare occasions are their apprentice works ever taken off the shelf, given a dusting and performed. Gluck, one of the greatest reformers, is remembered principally by his *Orpheus* and only two or three of his other operas are ever revived; Mozart actually composed twelve works for the stage in one form or another before he found his metier with his first masterpiece, *Idomeneo* (and apart from its glorious music, even that opera is not totally successful). The majority of the operas by Rossini, Donizetti and Bellini are rarely performed while Verdi's early operas up to *Macbeth* only occasionally see the light of day apart from *Nabucco*. Wagner's two very early attempts are rarely brought out of the cupboard and his third, *Rienzi* – modeled on the music of his bête noir, Meyerbeer – has met a similar fate. Puccini only discovered his personal idiom after three attempts, although in his first, *Le Villi*, there are glimpses of his later style; it was only after *Edgar* and the better but patchy *Manon Lescaut* that he truly succeeded with *La bohème*.

From the era of Puccini and Richard Strauss to the appearance of Britten, very few operas have survived the passage of time as a long list including Milhaud, Busoni, Hindemith, Pfitzner, Korngold, Respighi, Rutland Boughton, Vaughan Williams, Bruneau, Zandonai and countless others indicate. Genuine comic opera – without political or satirical implications – seems to have become extinct with the exception of Britten's classic chamber opera, *Albert Herring*, and even that masterpiece was sharply criticized as being devoid of humour when it first appeared. *Albert Herring* does have certain traces of caricature based on English upper-class respectability, but its portraits were painted with a soft brush rather than laid on with a heavy hand; after all, Lady Billows was modeled on Britten's benefactor, Joan Cross, and Florence on her housekeeper.

'*The best time to compose an overture*', Rossini wrote to an unknown composer, '*is to wait until the evening before opening night. Nothing primes inspiration more than necessity, whether it be the presence of a copyist waiting for your work or the prodding of an impresario tearing his hair. In my time, all the Italian impresarios were bald at thirty.*' Rossini had a reputation for extreme laziness and sometimes composed in bed so that when a page fell to the floor, rather than stretching down to retrieve it, he would write it out a second time (or even a third).

Church contra Theatre

In 1545, The Council of Trent ordained that bishops were '*to exclude music in which anything impious or lascivious finds a part*', so composers were no longer allowed to use the bawdy airs or street tunes on which they previously based their church music. Nevertheless many later composers — more familiarly associated with symphonic and operatic music — Haydn, Mozart, Rossini and Verdi being just a few, were naturally influenced by the church music in which they had been trained in their years of apprenticeship. Their mastery of church counterpoint and fugue inevitably spilled over into their operatic music while their music for the church was cross-fertilized by their operatic style. Rossini's *Stabat Mater* and his far from petite *Petite Messe Solennelle*, include arias and ensembles that could easily take their place in his comic operas and Verdi's *Messa di Requiem* and his other choral works are redolent of his highly theatrical operas. Likewise, the *Agnus Dei* in Mozart's *Coronation Mass* bears a resemblance to the Countess's third act aria, *Dove Sono*, in *Le nozze di Figaro*.

Operatic as Distinct from Symphonic Composition

As the music in an opera mirrors the text, it may require frequent changes of tempo to match changing dramatic situations, so the layout for an operatic full score is quite different to that for a symphony. The majority of pre-twentieth-century operas include recitatives punctuated by orchestral chords; the orchestra may be silent for many bars and have to hold pauses so that singers can show off their top notes or to allow for entrances and exits. This may not appear to be that much different to symphonic writing which continuously flows, but in opera the conductor and the orchestra have to have greater flexibility and be aware of what is happening on stage at any moment. An opera's playing time may be short — twenty minutes

(Milhaud) to over four hours (Mozart and Wagner) – but a concert programme lasts approximately two hours with music by as many as four or five composers – each with their own individual style – whereas an opera has only one particular composer's musical personality. Another important factor is that a concert programme is performed once only (occasionally repeated) whereas an opera may have as many as ten or more performances.

It is also imperative for conductors to be have a knowledge of stylistic differences which are no more apparent than between the music of Mozart and Wagner. Mozart inherited the baroque concept in which each note 'decayed', partly derived from the lack of vibrato in their string playing and partly from the harpsichord's mechanical action. In the baroque period, no keyboard instrument was able to sustain the sound once the note was struck because the strings were plucked rather than hammered as was the case for the the later pianoforte, or in German, *hammerklavier*. During the latter part of Mozart's life the baroque techniques began to wane as a result of larger theatres being built that demanded more resonance. Then in the nineteenth century, orchestra pits were constructed which again compelled musicians to find a way for the instruments to resonate at a greater intensity to penetrate much further into the auditorium. Consequently, violin chin-rests were invented so that the string players could hold their instruments firmly while allowing their left hands the freedom to produce a vibrato. Later composers and Wagner in particular all benefited from this new technique in the quest for a perpetual legato to enhance their polyphonic writing for the orchestra. Only from the latter half of the twentieth century and the revival of the older instruments could something of the eighteenth-century sound be once again experienced (which came as a revelation). As all students of history are aware, new ideas are often greeted negatively so some of the older maestri who had inherited Wagner's principles found it difficult to accept the new (old) absence of vibrato.

Librettists

Benedetto Marcello penned some tongue-in-cheek satirical remarks about librettists in his *Il teatro alla moda* of 1720. '*A writer of operatic libretti, if he wishes to be modern must not have read the Greek or Latin classic authors, nor should he do so in the future. After all, the old Greek and Romans never read modern writers . . . He should, on the other hand, boast that he has had thorough schooling in mathematics, painting, chemistry, medicine, law, etc. and should then confess that his genius so strongly compelled him to it, that he just had to become a poet . . . he would write the entire opera without preconceived plan, but rather proceed verse by verse. For, if the audience never understands the plot, it can be counted on to be attentive to the very end . . . He should conclude with the customary chorus in praise of the sun, moon, or impresario.*' Verdi, however, expressed his difficulty in finding a good collaborator in two succinct sentences: '*I read with reluctance the librettos that are sent to me. It is impossible, or almost impossible for someone else to divine what I want.*' In more recent times, Leos Janáček had equally pertinent comments on the setting of texts as his vocal writing specifically depended on the rise and fall and inflection of the Czech language: '*On the stage, it is not always the best word for vocalizing that we require; we need the everyday word, its melodic turn, torn from life, misery congealed, despair in sharp relief. Real life is needed in opera.*'

A librettist has to accept the potentially embarrassing situation of being a subservient collaborator rather than being the sole creator and, whether a superb prose writer or a first-class poet, it is not necessarily sufficient qualification to write a libretto. Yet librettists should not consider their work as simply inferior literature or second-rate drama. In fact, Hugo von Hofmannsthal, Richard Strauss's collaborator, was a particularly fine writer of prose and a dramatist in his own right but believed that writing a good libretto was much more difficult than writing a play.

One of the first librettists still remembered today was the Abbé Metastasio (Pietro Trapassi) a grocer's son who was adopted by a wealthy patron whose vast wealth he inherited. Metastasio died in Vienna – where he had been the court poet for half a century – at the ripe old age of eighty-four, having become the most celebrated librettist in Europe. His librettos were considered the acme of perfection and set by many of the most notable composers of the day including Handel, Gluck, Haydn and Johann Adolph Hasse, the latter setting every one of his texts once, and some even twice. Mozart set four of Metastasio's librettos, *Il sogno di Scipione, Lucio Silla, Il rè Pastore* and *La clemenza di Tito*.

At that time, the rules for good libretto writing were that it had to include six characters who were in love; the three major principals were to be sung by a castrato, a prima donna, and a tenor, all of whom had to have five arias – a *l'aria patetica* (an outburst of passion), an *aria di bravura* (with technical virtuosity), an *aria parlante* (in a sustained style), an example of *demi-caractè* and an *aria brillante* (unrestrained joy and happiness). The text should not exceed a specified number of lines, and the opera had to be written in three acts; each scene had to conclude with an aria; no one character should sing two arias in succession and no two arias in the same category should follow each other. Acts I and 2 had to conclude with impressive arias but totally different in character to any of the other arias. In the second act, there had to be a *Recitativo obligato* followed by an *aria di trambusto* (in the Grand Manner) and a heroic duet for the leading pair of lovers; yet despite all these incredible restrictions, the opera had to end happily!

The arias mentioned above were just a few of a veritable lexicon compiled to cover many, if not all, eventualities.

Aria Cantabile – a slow and smooth aria that allowed for embellishment, usually in the reprise (Da Capo) of the first section.

Aria di portamento – often composed in long notes and not to be embellished so that it could be sung with a smooth delivery between notes with a crescendo and a decrescendo on each; hence *portamento* (to carry).

Aria di mezzo carattere or *Aria parlante* – to be declaimed (spoken on pitch) rather than sung.

Aria di bravura (d'agilità or *d'abilità)* – to be performed with boldness and/or agility.

Aria all'unisono – the accompaniment in octaves or unison with the voice. *'The people that walk in darkness'* in Handel's *Messiah* is one of a very few such arias still performed today.

Aria d'imitazione – depicting birds, hunting horns and other extra-musical sounds.

Aria concertante – with instrumental obligato.

Aria senza accompagnamento – an unaccompanied aria.

Aria d'entrata – the first aria to be sung on entering.

Aria fugata – an aria with fugal accompaniment.

Aria tedesca – in the German rather than the Italian style (i.e. less showy).

Aria aggiunta – an aria added after the completion of the opera to satisfy a particular singer or an unsatisfied audience.

Lorenzo da Ponte was a librettist for a number of Viennese composers but unfortunately for posterity, he collaborated with Mozart only three times. After *Così fan tutte* the machinations against his mistress by her colleagues in the Vienna Opera compelled him to flee so he escaped to America where he became the proprietor of a liquor and hardware store, and opened a finishing school for young ladies. Some later librettists like Scribe, Meilhac and Halévy threw off texts at the drop of a hat for any composer in need, but there have also been splendid collaborations, especially that of Verdi with Boito and Richard Strauss with Hugo von Hofmannsthal. Puccini had innumerable problems with his librettists and even resorted to three for *La bohème*, who between them somehow managed to collaborate to provide

Puccini with what he wanted. *La bohème* was originally in five acts but scissors and paste became the order of the day and its four acts are now the epitome of expressive conciseness! Only a few composers have written their own librettos, the most well known being Wagner and Tippett. Wagner's operatic texts, like his literary articles, are frequently convoluted, and Tippett's are sometimes embarrassingly gauche.

*T*ranslations

Few English-speaking playgoers expect surtitles in the theatre for Chekhov in Russian and Ibsen in Norwegian, but subtitles are the accepted norm for foreign films. Paradoxically, their operatic counterparts only tolerate opera in its original language even though a large proportion of the public have little or no knowledge of languages other than their own. There is probably an element of snobbery in this attitude as, until relatively recently, even in such operatically sophisticated countries as Germany and Italy, Wagner in Italy was usually performed in translation, and likewise, Verdi in Germany. Should opera continue into the future in its present form, in Voltaire's 'best of all possible (operatic) worlds', there ought to be room made for performances in both the original language and in translation.

Translating a text presents enormous problems of scansion and inflexion: German to English is not so much of a problem, but French to English is quite difficult to bring off well, and Italian to English is relatively easy even though English has more hard consonants. Although the repetition of words when sung in an Italian nineteenth-century opera may sound perfectly natural to an Anglo-Saxon, in English it can be comical for the wrong reasons unless the singer is able to inflect each repetition differently. Until recently many English singers accepted banal translations, outmoded idioms and rhyming doggerel without question, or they were simply ignorant of the original language, but that is rarely the case today. No self-respecting singer would dare to sing a translation without a thorough understanding of each word and line of the original. A good translation can convey the emotional content of the original even if the new text does not keep to a literal equivalent.

Whereas original librettos do not need to be brought up to date there are a few exceptions, as in Mozart's German operas in which the original language has changed since Mozart's day; translations, on the other hand, need to be revised for every generation. Many of the older editions of vocal scores are spattered with words like 'thee' and 'thou' and other gibberish left over from the Victorian age. Arguably the most amusing case of the tyranny of rhyme over reason that was sung until quite recently was in Saint-Saëns' *Samson et Dalila*: *'He lay there a gasping, she his weapon grasping'* – fortunately that line has gone the way of all flesh!

The Re-Creators

Haydn, Mozart, Berlioz, Wagner and most other composers conducted their own music as a matter of course, but since the creation of the Bayreuth myth that the composer must be worshipped as a divine right, conductors and other performers have been indoctrinated with the belief that they are the composer's servants. To a certain extent that is true, and whether alive or dead, composers should be treated with respect and the utmost humility, but creators are completely helpless without executants who bring their work to life, so neither can express themselves without the other. Performers, on the other hand, need to be aware of the cultural and technical parameters of the composer's period and style, but thereafter the work's re-creation develops out of the performer's own personality and experience. This master/servant relationship has also influenced some performers into believing that the printed page is the equivalent of a cooking recipe or an industrial blueprint and interpreted accordingly, but a score should really be considered as a musical reflection of the ideas that emanate from it.

Musical Director / Conductor

At the pinnacle of the operatic pyramid is the Musical Director who, by inference, is also the Artistic Director for the simple fact that an opera's dramatic timing and visual character should stem from the music — its tempo, melodic and harmonic shape and its rhythm. More often than not the Musical Director is also a conductor whose duties not only include conducting a major portion of the repertoire, but also the selection of the repertoire, casting and choice of producer; in fact, generally overseeing the company's artistic purpose and goals along with the General Manager. A busy conducting career elsewhere also demands hectic travel arrangements so an MD is often absent from the day-to-day running of the company, unlike Mahler, Toscanini and Bruno Walter who watched over their companies for considerable periods. There are exceptions of course; James Levine at the Metropolitan, and Gergiev at the Bolshoi amongst them, but even they spend less time with their respective companies than did their predecessors. In the past some Musical Directors tended to be tyrannical and decidedly autocratic but — with the advent of the musician's union and the necessity for good industrial relations — they have now become quasi benevolent dictators with the company's resident singers and orchestra all involved in the artistic well-being of their company.

At one time virtually every great conductor served a valuable apprenticeship period as a repetiteur, but surprisingly not every MD today can play the piano. This can be a drawback, as working as a repetiteur in an opera company is an excellent way to gain all-round conducting experience. Back-stage, this may range from cueing a solitary horn in Act 3 of *Falstaff* to conducting a complete Viennese café orchestra in *Der Rosenkavalier*, the stage-band in *Don Giovanni* and many choral interjections. It may also entail using a torch in total darkness and following the principal conductor on a television monitor (previously, a spy hole in the scenery). The monitor has another useful function in that it provides a unique opportunity to observe different conductors from the player's perspective. The natural progression for the fledgling maestro is then to conduct production rehearsals – with piano accompaniment – and later, one or two of the stage with orchestra rehearsals in the pit. This usually leads to taking over the conducting of performances, often with little or no orchestral rehearsal; it is always a challenge for he or she has the responsibility without the authority for the performance. This time honoured *gradus ad Parnassum* inevitably develops good baton technique and general musicianship and, if a strong personality emanates in the process, the possibility of becoming a fully-fledged conductor.

The popular idea that the conductor is in touch with the infinite at all times and totally disinterested in mundane matters is belied by the exactness needed when planning rehearsals so as to achieve maximum results in the (often too little) allocated time. The conductor must have a precise estimation of the time needed for each work based on a variety of factors: duration, complexity and/or unfamiliarity for the orchestra. However, should a rehearsal finish early because it has gone well, a later rehearsal cannot be extended as a return favour without the payment of overtime. The conductor should also decide on the rehearsals that require extra players, such as a third percussionist, a contra-bassoonist or a harpist who may only be needed for one aria. By such careful considerations an astute conductor can save the management considerable expense and earn the gratitude of the players because they can then accept outside engagements to augment their income.

Conducting is a mystery that cannot be explained logically and consequently the art and craft is sometimes open to ridicule. In

1890, a London newspaper included an article under the title of Musical Imposters. *'The definition of a conductor is a man who describes form in the air with a stick or wand and who expects, nay demands all those before him to be subject and subordinate to him. He is the one man producing nothing musically but claiming to produce all things. Is the conductor only a self-elected acrobat who has cajoled a number of persons to believe in his assumed necessity? Is conducting the resort of those who have no speciality as instrumental or vocal performer? In short, is a conductor an ass in a lion's skin? The conductor is a useless excrescence of quite modern growth.'* One can only assume that the tongue-in-cheek writer was referring to symphonic baton wavers rather than their operatic colleagues.

As with every other artistic discipline, the need for ambition coupled with determination is the keystone to a successful conducting career, which is no more exemplified than in a supposed incident between Toscanini and the cellist Piatigorsky. The Maestro rounded on the cellist just before going on the concert platform with the explosion 'you are an appalling cellist, you lack rhythm and phrasing and you are hopeless at following me. I, on the other hand cannot control the orchestra, I am tone-deaf and a hopeless conductor, especially in Verdi and Puccini. However, there is no one better than us, is there!' The moral of this little fable is that a conductor must have a combination of complete self-confidence and total humility!

Producer / Director

A Producer, sometimes designated State Director, may be very musical yet have little musicianship, so this subtle distinction needs qualification. Musicianship implies the ability to read music, a reasonable knowledge of theory and some practical ability at the keyboard, a stringed or woodwind instrument, or singing. Even if those skills are in abundance, a producer may still be fundamentally unmusical whereas one with a little or no musicianship can still sense the dramatic meaning behind the notes – its *melos* (melody in Greek), hence *melo-drama*, the original name for what later became opera.

Some producers start at the bottom rung of the professional ladder as Assistant Stage-Managers and work their way up through the various technical departments gaining much practical experience on the way. Others come to opera from the 'straight' theatre having been invited to produce an experimental work or to create a novel inter-pretation for a sure-fire popular opera; management can then assess their ability in the totally different world of *'exotic entertainment'*.

When producers, unfamiliar with opera, are interviewed by the media, some regurgitate platitudes based on little or no experience as to what the designation 'opera' means – music, drama, singing and gesture fused in one expressive entity; through ignorance they imply that opera is really drama which is spoilt by music and ham-fisted singers. It must be admitted that some operas have flimsy subjects but they are camouflaged with marvellous music as for instance, a few – but by no means all – *bel canto* operas. But a musical producer can create exciting backdrops for beautiful singing. When a producer keeps within traditional boundaries, the production is often criticized as unimaginative, unspectacular or irrelevant, yet if its is a 'post-modern' conception, it is vehemently attacked by those who demand that tradi-tion is sacrosanct!

The Conductor–Producer Relationship

The nature of opera as described above implies that two direc-tors are required – a conductor and a producer. But if their artistic intentions should differ, the most destructive situation in opera arises, incompatibility. Feuds quickly develop which then spill over into the actual rehearsals so that the singers become unsettled and their confi-dence badly undermined, causing considerable embarrassment all round. There have been a number of instances when conductors have produced and conducted at the same time, but the result is often unsuccessful because the singers don't have the producer's guiding hand during the final period of stage with orchestra rehearsals.

When production rehearsals are under way it can be extremely annoying if a conductor persistently interrupts the producer to correct musical slips or demand the staging to be changed because of a lack of visual contact or difficulty in controlling the vocal ensemble. If the conductor draws the producer's attention to the problem early in the proceedings, the response is likely to be that the production is still in an embryonic stage; yet if the conductor is tactful and raises the matter later, he or she is likely to be rebuked for failing to point out the problem earlier! It is imperative that a good working relationship is established before rehearsals commence, though difficulties as mentioned above are not necessarily one-sided. Some conductors adopt extreme tempos and even fluctuate from one rehearsal to another such that they cause entrances and exits to be timed badly or the character interplay to be completely upset. However, when the two directors are compatible, then rehearsals can be an exhilarating experience for all concerned.

Opera Ballet / Dance / Movement

Dance has always had a place in one form of performance or another involving music, as for instance, the Masque, Purcell's *Dido & Aeneas* which included witches dances, and Mozart's conclusion to Act I of *Idomeneo* with a ballet sequence under the heading of Ciaccona. The dances most frequently used in opera are the Menuetto (*Don Giovanni*), Fandango (*Le nozze di Figaro*), Gavotte (*Manon*), Waltz (*Fledermaus*), Polonaise and Mazurka (*Eugene Onegin*) and Polka (*The Bartered Bride*). The Menuetto in *Don Giovanni* is actually juxtaposed with both a Country dance and a German dance and although the score of *Le nozze di Figaro* states Fandango during the Finale of Act 3, it is unlike the modern fandango and rather more like a minuet. Twentieth-century composers such as Richard Strauss, Michael Tippett and Benjamin Britten all incorporated various dance movements into their operas, especially in *Salome*, *Intermezzo*, *The Midsummer Marriage*, *Gloriana* and *Death in Venice*. Many operas include scenes in which the singers dance as part of the dramatic action, like the Polonaise, Mazurka and Ecossaise in Tchaikovsky's *Eugene Onegin*. But some companies employ professional dancers for these scenes; unfortunately they can stand out from the rest of the cast and spoil the dramatic truth.

Movement classes are very beneficial for singers to help focus their attention on unnecessary arm and hand gestures, which they (mistakenly) believe help their vocal emission. Many opera singers are ignorant of how deportment and poise actually encourage good singing. Some opera companies now encourage their singers to practise the Alexander Technique to promote a natural rhythm between their singing and movement.

The Designer

The designer is usually chosen by the producer for the obvious reason that the stage setting is very much in the producer's domain. When a new production is being contemplated, the design discussions usually include the Musical Director/Conductor and the General Manager. Conductors are not always able to participate due to other commitments but it is too late for them to protest about an opera's design after the sets have been approved and well on the way to being constructed.

Designing an opera has to encompass any number of practicalities, especially scene changes. For instance, the set for Beethoven's *Fidelio* has to be changed very quickly – from Florestan's claustrophobic dungeon to a large outdoor square in Seville, big enough to contain a large chorus and principal singers. Mahler was in the habit of conducting the Leonore No. 3 Overture to cover the time it took to change the set, but dramatically it was totally wrong; halfway through the act, the off-stage trumpet had already heralded the arrival of the Minister to release Florestan and then the playing of the Overture included the same musical sequence! Another example is the very short second act of *La bohème* (15–20 minutes depending on the conductor's tempo), set in and around the Café Momus. The change of set from the attic in Act I, to an open-fronted café and the street, large enough to contain a big chorus, eight principals and many extras, has to be carried out very quickly.

The Drottningholm Court Theatre in Sweden still uses the thirty original baroque sets which can be changed in as little as ten seconds using a pulley system under the stage. Gods and Goddesses are able to descend in chariots, or float on clouds; creatures from the nether regions can appear out of the floor; rolling waves are simulated by using winches and pulleys; and thunder is created by rolling an enormous stone ball on the wooden floor. The materials used for set construction also affect the acoustics so where wood predominates (as in Drottningholm), the sets act as a sounding board (rather like the belly of a Stradivarius violin). Open sets using steel and other metals may not be nearly so good. Many singers dislike an open stage, finding it unhelpful and vocally unflattering. Theatrical holograms are still at the experimental stage and something of a 'new toy' but eventually they may save considerable building costs as well as cumbersome sets.

The Lighting Designer is a relative newcomer to the production team. Indeed, prior to the 1950s, the producer, assisted by a technical operator, usually conceived the lighting, but it has now become an art in its own right.

*T*echnical Departments

Set building is usually the responsibility of an in-house staff who on occasion may need as much as a year to construct a highly complex set, but some companies prefer to contract outside organizations. The set has not only to be visually satisfying, but – if the production is successful – it needs to be sturdy to survive for a considerable time and stand the wear and tear of possible national and international tours. A typical rehearsal schedule will involve the erection and dismantling of a set in the morning, repeating the process with a different set for another opera for the evening performance, and then repeating the pattern as one opera finishes and another takes its place in the season. Operas with orchestral interludes between scenes need the sets to be changed in complete silence, especially when the orchestra is playing as softly and delicately as in Debussy's *Pelléas et Mélisande.*

The Wardrobe is busy all year round making costumes, keeping them in good repair, and adapting them when necessary for different performers and revivals. The wear and tear during the course of any one season is considerable and as a singer's physical and mental exertions can cause a lot of perspiration, regular cleaning and repair is an important chore. Exactly timed wardrobe fittings are also essential during the production rehearsals for, if a singer is suddenly unavailable, the producer's plans are totally disrupted much to everyone's annoyance. A heavy costume is another problem: singers must be able to breathe and move easily or dehydration will affect their metabolism and ability to perform. The rôle of Falstaff is the classic example in that it must give the impression of the knight's rotundity, yet the padding cannot be too heavy to carry around during a performance that lasts approximately three hours; taking the padding off during the Intervals is a relief. It has been known for producers to demand real nineteenth-century corsets for oversize sopranos and then, despite a great deal of remonstration, to pull in the binding strings very tight; historically correct but detrimental to good singing.

The Perruquier or Perruquière (female) makes and maintains the wigs and the highly elaborate eighteenth-century coiffures of both male and female characters. This may entail many hours at the block to produce wigs for the entire Russian court in Act 2 of Tchaikovsky's *Pikova Dama* (The Queen of Spades), but arguably the most difficult hairpiece of all is for Melisande in Debussy's opera. At the beginning of Act 3, her hair is expected to cascade from a window high up in Arkel's castle all the way to Pelleas down in the garden who sensually entwines himself in it – a major problem for both the producer and the perruquier who often need a soupçon of poetic license to disguise the real length of her tresses.

Make-up has also become an expert's prerogative. Although basic make-up is left to each individual singer, some operas require exotic applications, as for instance Japanese in *Madama Butterfly* and Chinese for *Turandot*. In the Egyptian world of Mozart's *Die Zauberflöte*, Monastatos is black and consequently may need a complete body make-up, but somehow ways are found to cope with this arduous and time-consuming problem.

With the technicalities involved in opera becoming more and more complex, Production Managers are now vitally necessary to co-ordinate, not only one production, but also how it slots into the repertoire in any one season and later revivals. The Production Manager's responsibilities also have to include every aspect of the day-to-day running of the company. This individual needs to keep an ear open to the theatrical grapevine in order to contract new personnel for all the technical departments.

Stage Managers need to have the right sort of personality to cope with the emergencies that regularly happen in opera. Before every performance they make sure that the lighting system functions on cue and that the set is undamaged (despite the inevitable manhandling). During the performance, they are responsible for the running of the opera from their position in the corner, ensuring that the principals and chorus are ready in the wings; 'temperamental' artists are under control (in the nicest possible way); lighting cues are given; and difficult entrances and exits and rapid costume changes are overseen in the wings. Unlike their straight theatre colleagues, they must also be able to follow a vocal score in a foreign language, which can be difficult if the score is very complex or extremely fast. And all the time, his or her eyes and ears have to be on the stage, back stage and in the orchestra pit.

Prior to the twentieth century the Stage Manager produced revivals, but in more recent times the position of Assistant Producer has proved to be necessary because the original producer may not be available or is perhaps uninterested in supervising a revival. Like an assistant conductor, he or she has the responsibility without authority to make or agree to any changes requested by new singers to the production. To make some small alterations is not wrong, as any performer must be as psychologically compatible with the rôle as was the original creator, but if the new singer for the revival indulges in autocratic, prima donna attitudes, tensions easily ensue. When a great deal of the production is altered at their behest, it becomes virtually a new conception and some original creators have withdrawn their names from the production as a consequence.

Repertoire

Curiously, the most popular operas also have *exotic* plots – partly because opera is larger than life – but it is question of opinion as to whether their plots are irrelevant in contemporary terms. The list includes:

La bohème – bohemianism and terminal illness.

Aida – jealousy and live burial.

La traviata – terminal illness and emotional blackmail.

Rigoletto – deformity, and abduction for sexual purposes.

Il trovatore – child abduction and witchcraft.

Madama Butterfly – bigamy, suicide and racial discrimination.

Tosca – attempted rape, political assassination and suicide.

Carmen – seduction, murder and cigarette manufacture.

Don Giovanni – attempted rape, murder, wife abandonment and
talking statues.

Le nozze di Figaro – feudal custom versus human rights.

Die Zauberflöte – the struggle between good and evil and the
supernatural.

Così fan tutte – potential wife swapping.

Die Fledermaus – adultery, drunkenness, decadence with a hint
of lesbianism.

Il barbiere di Seviglia – elopement and intrigue.

Der Rosenkavalier – sexual dalliance with a much younger male
(sung by a female) and the aging process.

Faust – the impossible search for everlasting youth aided and
abetted by the devil.

The less popular operas include such masterpieces as *Ariadne auf Naxos, Falstaff, Otello, Eugene Onegin, Werther, The Rake's Progress, Peter Grimes, Billy Budd, Pelleas & Melisande* and *L'incoronazione di Poppea*, with Wagner's music dramas, in a unique category of their own, inspiring obsessive adulation and frequent long-distance travel. In the past, it was felt that Operetta, Musical Comedy and the American Musical – renamed Music Theatre – were beneath the dignity of respectable opera houses but with box-office survival more of a necessity than ever before, companies have had to change such antiquated attitudes. Many companies now include such splendid works as *My Fair Lady, Oklahoma, Fiddler on the Roof* and *Kiss me Kate*. But house conductors and singers schooled in the *bel canto* tradition who have a flair for the genre are not so plentiful, and only a few conductors manage to bridge the great divide between 'popular' music and opera.

Planning a season's repertoire requires a careful balance between artistic value and financial success, which in turn depend on fairly complex practical considerations. Audience numbers will soon diminish if, during a subscription series, any one opera is scheduled too often or there is an imbalance between the most popular Italian and German repertoire. Revivals have to be considered, and sometimes before a new production has even achieved its hoped-for success, guest artists have to be re-engaged before they are contracted elsewhere. The selection of a repertoire usually tries to include a guest 'star' to provide status and to attract a larger audience but it is frustrating when such a star – around whom a new production has been created – withdraws at a late stage in the planning. Casting a new opera with a famous star in the title rôle is not as straightforward as it would seem because finding 'stars' willing to learn difficult new works – usually for only a few performances – is difficult, especially if they have to forego seasons elsewhere in their famous rôles where they need only minimal prepa-ration and rehearsals. Another complication when choosing the repertoire is the likely incompatibility between artists, be they singer and conductor, singer and producer, conductor and producer, or any other permutation. Inevitably, the determining factor is the box-office appeal of one over the other.

In a Stagione (seasonal) company with a limited number of singers in each *fach* (vocal category), choice of repertoire also has to take into account the resident singer's vocal and physical stamina. He or she should not be expected to perform more than four times a week at the very most – usually three – especially if they are rehearsing another opera on the morning of a performance. This is normally understood for all but the smallest rôles, but three performances of a heavy one such as Rigoletto with morning rehearsals of Don Giovanni or Leporello is just about the limit for any baritone. Multiplying this permutation across the company's roster and taking into consideration the conductor's availability is a complicated exercise in logistics.

Casting

Operatic casting is inevitably different from casting in the theatre because rôles such as Verdi's Macbeth and Otello can only be sung by one very specific type of baritone and tenor, whereas Shakespeare's Macbeth and Othello can be cast from any number of actors. Narrowing the possibilities even further, a particular baritone may be dramatically suitable but vocally inadequate or vice versa. This sort of situation was instrumental in evolving the German *fach* system in which singers are carefully categorized. However, sometimes singers have to move from one *fach* to another when changes occur to their vocal cords due to various physical developments; voices can rise or become heavier and darker in the course of time, usually through regular usage, although it is rare for voices to fall or lighten. A change of fach requires having to learn a completely new repertoire so the singers might have to opt out of performing for a while, which complicates matters if they have been contracted two or three years prior to the start of rehearsals (as is now common practice). Assuming that no fach changes occur, a cast may still turn out to be vocally different to that originally planned especially if a singer's vocal prowess has diminished during the interim period. Another problem, which may not be apparent when planning a season, is that a few years later when they come together for the first time, a superb cast on paper may not jell, vocally or otherwise. But when the ensemble does turn out to be greater than the sum of its individual parts and creates an exhilarating performance, it makes the precariousness of opera planning eminently worthwhile.

It took a considerable time for racial discrimination and colour prejudice to be totally eliminated from the international world of opera but it is now accepted practice — even when historically incorrect — to cast any rôle with black singers. Productions of *Die Zauberflöte* have included a black Tamino even though the Monostatos (representing the darker side of humanity) was also black. Bayreuth has cast many black singers in *The Ring* despite Wagner's virulent racialism, and Strauss's *Der Rosenkavalier* has had a black mezzo-soprano as Octavian, the young Viennese nobleman, which would not have been possible in the era of Maria Theresa.

The Conducting Roster

Once upon a time, a lady entered a pet shop with the intention of buying an exotic bird. 'How much is that one, and what can it do?' she asked. 'It can sing Tamino in German and Rudolfo in Italian and is priced at $10,000.' 'Any others?' asked the buyer. 'Yes, this one which is much more beautiful and can sing Wagner's complete Ring cycle but its price is $25,000.' Then the lady spotted a mangy, dull and bedraggled little bird huddled in the corner. 'You must be giving that one away, it looks so pitiful?' 'Oh no, it is the most expensive bird we have and you would get little change from $50,000!' The astounded lady could only blurt out, 'What does it do that is costs so much?' The shopkeeper replied, 'Well, nobody really knows, but it's always flapping its wings about, shouting at everyone and commands them all to address him as "Maestro"!'

In countries, especially those with an Italian orientation, conductors are addressed respectfully as *Maestro* (Master), and in Germany as *Meister, Docktor* or *Dirigent* and — if subordinate to the Musical Director — *Erste Kapellmeister*. In France the conductor is hailed as Chef, but in England, the down-to-earth approach of *Mister* is heard. In Australia, however, where doctors and surgeons are regularly addressed by their first names, young singers unfamiliar with the tradition have been known to address the conductor with the same good-natured salute, although such bonhomie is not always received favourably by visiting maestri!

The conducting roster has usually a maximum of four plus an assistant conductor. Conductors are allotted ample rehearsal time for new productions but it is now common practice to dispense with an equivalent period for revivals even though the conductor may be conducting the opera for the first time. The shorter rehearsal schedule is based on the assumption that the singers and the orchestra are conversant with the opera so that a complete rehearsal schedule is unnecessary. It frequently means that the cast only meet the new conductor at one, or occasionally two production rehearsals, followed by one orchestral rehearsal or none at all. Alternatively, a new conductor may have one orchestral rehearsal but have no contact with the singers until the actual performance.

*F*emale Conductors

Female conductors began to make their presence felt from the early years of the twentieth century, but only recently have they begun to be fully accepted on the rostrum. In England, one of the first was the eccentric Dame Ethel Smyth, who on one occasion, conducted a choir of suffragettes with a toothbrush. Despite this episode, she was also a composer of some eminence with a number of operas to her credit. *The Boatswain's Mate* is an excellent, one-act comic opera that deserves to be occasionally revived; *The Wreckers* was premièred at Covent Garden and is said to have been a model for Britten's *Peter Grimes*. A slightly later period saw the emergence of other female conductors, such as Avril Coleridge-Taylor, the daughter of the composer of *Hiawatha's Wedding Feast* and Imogen Holst, who like her father, Gustav, inspired many amateur music makers without detriment to their work with professionals. Ethel Liggins assumed the surname of Leginska and wore men's clothes to disguise her femininity in front of the orchestra; Antonia Brico from Holland was the first woman to conduct the Berlin Philharmonic Orchestra but was dismissed from the Metropolitan Opera in New York when a baritone refused to sing under a woman! The American, Judith Somogi, was appointed Kapellmeister in Frankfurt and maintained that women could better succeed in opera than on the concert platform because they would be less visible. The next generation included Sarah Caldwell who was very successful in Boston where she conducted the American premières of such rarities as *Les Troyens* and *Moses und Aron*, as neither were in the standard repertoire at the time. In France, Jane Evrandin made a good impression and more recently, Nadia Boulanger has been a tremendous influence on the revival of Monteverdi besides grooming many young composers including Aaron Copland, Lennox Berkeley and Thea Musgrave.

The 'gentlemen's agreement' against female conductors gradually disappeared with more and more coming forward, such as Jane Glover, Sean Edwards and Simone Young. The latter was initially ignored by her *alma mater* in Sydney but was the first female conductor with enough audacity to face that most male chauvinistic orchestra, the Vienna Philharmonic. She was later appointed Musical Director of Opera Australia, the very company that had previously ignored her. The days have long gone since someone of the calibre of Sir Thomas Beecham could quip that if a female musician was unattractive she was not wanted near an orchestra, but if she was beautiful it would be too distracting!

*T*he Conductor in the Pit

An opera orchestra has its own administration quite independent of the opera company's management to cope with the day-to-day requirements of the players as well as the comings and goings in the orchestra pit. Keeping the pit in good condition involves an enormous amount of time and energy, not only in maintenance, but in repositioning chairs and stands for morning rehearsals, evening performances, and for different configurations the following day.

'Pit' is a little demeaning yet it is difficult to suggest any alternative other than the "black hole of . . . " as it is affectionately nicknamed by some musicians! Although the Bayreuth pit remains the ideal model for any new pit, the players themselves experience reverberation problems and cannot always judge their own dynamics accurately or hear their colleagues, never mind the singers on stage – despite the superb sound that emanates.

Bayreuth is recognized as the epitome of what an opera pit should be, but it was Verdi in fact who modernized the seating for the première of his *Otello*. Up to that time the brass section had actually been behind the conductor's back and played towards the stage. It probably influenced Donizetti's surprisingly heavy brass writing in his comic operas for, by the time the brass *fff* reached the audience, it had diminished to a comfortable *mf* despite the singers experiencing the full blast!

When orchestras were considerably smaller and before orchestra pits were even imagined, there were never any contact or balance problems with the singers, but the introduction of sunken pits created occupational hazards for the musicians. In the larger and older theatres built during the nineteenth century these problems are minimal, but adequate space is vital for string players to bow and trombonists to operate their slides; similarly horns need plenty of space behind their bells to resonate. The reverberation in some boxed-in pits has now begun to affect the hearing loss of conductors and players alike, even before the normal ageing process begins to take its toll. These are the facts of life for those who spend their working lives in the 'black hole' so it is not surprising that some musicians are averse to working in opera orchestras. They also have to be aware of flying objects from the stage. Most opera houses now have nets strung across the pit above the musicians to catch any missiles. Unfortunately the net often lies right across the conductor's line of vision. For some modern productions, conductors have to accept a catwalk behind their backs, as in the American Vaudeville of the 1930s so that the singers can have an intimacy with the audience.

In Germany, a number of performances of a particular opera may spread over many months, and, with the standard repertoire endlessly repeated, it can easily lead to the adoption of a blasé attitude as instanced by the author when deputizing for a sick colleague. A composer friend moonlighting in the viola section asked, 'What are you doing here?' I replied, 'Conducting of course'. But when the same question was put to him, his instinctive answer was, 'Oh, we never look at the conductor in *Die Zauberflöte* and anyway, conductors come and go all the time'! A long season presents the conductor with the problem of maintaining the players' enthusiasm throughout, especially as the majority of them are likely to have played the operas many times before. If the excitement and adrenaline of the opening night is not being continuously rejuvenated, boredom can easily set in. This ever recurring fact of pit life was fictitiously described by Berlioz in his *Les Soirées de l'orchestre*, in twenty-five evenings during which the players overcome their boredom with humorous and rather more serious stories. On the evenings when their favourite masterpieces were performed, however, the players concentrated furiously.

It is a common fallacy among conductors that they need large, high gestures in the pit; in fact, small gestures actually compel singers to focus on what is happening down below, as well as being more precise in the relative darkness. The number of television monitors in the wings or suspended above the stage have helped to solve the problem of contact but it must be quite galling for an irascible Diva to have six or seven conductor-clones all gesticulating at her from every direction, and, to make matters worse, in perfect ensemble! Singers tend to think of the conductor as a glorified accompanist but this error of judgement has to be corrected from time to time; naturally the conductor should be sympathetic, but the opera is literally in the conductor's hands rather than the singer's.

Cast changes also present problems for both conductor and orchestra as one singer may need a fraction more time to breath than another, phrase differently, or suddenly make a pause in an unexpected place. As previously mentioned, some conductors are unaware of the importance of breathing and when such conductors are let loose in a pit, it can be catastrophic for the singers in their charge. Split-second reactions and decisions are sometimes necessary, especially when a singer fails to materialize on stage or, as happened on one occasion at Sadlers Wells many years ago, Cho-Cho-San's house in *Madama Butterfly* folded in on itself like a pack of cards! Conductors ought to be the humblest of egocentric megalomaniacs but if they ever stopped to think of the artistic and financial responsibility that is dependent on the point of their batons, high blood pressure or even worse calamities might result!

Health, Hearing Loss and Physical Stamina

Although physical fitness is universally recognized as very important, few conductors seem to be concerned about their health and well-being, believing perhaps in the myth that they are, by nature, long-lived. This may be true to a certain degree by the number of old maestri, although those that die young are quickly forgotten as they hardly have an opportunity to make much of an impression! Certainly the physical exercise involved in conducting is beneficial but it tends to affect the body above the waist rather than below and, should conductors move their arms around without any musical stimulation, the physical exertion would almost certainly induce heart failure. Conductors tend not to eat before a concert, but the loss of so much body fluid and energy during a performance means that they often relax afterwards by over-eating and drinking. A conductor's posture is also important; standing for three or more hours creates a tremendous downward pressure on the feet. In the pit (hidden from the audience), one way of alleviating the problem is by shaking each foot from time to time so that the blood circulates (though the orchestra may be highly amused by the conductor's peculiar behaviour).

The effect of physical and mental stress on the conductor was researched at The Institute of Fitness in Adelaide, South Australia in the 1970s. The conductor concerned first studied the score in private, then he was observed during rehearsals, and finally at the concert. It was assumed that conducting the opera would produce a similar result, perhaps even more so due to its greater all-round complexity. *The results may not be applicable to every conductor but nevertheless provide a valuable insight into the nature of a conductor's physical and mental state during a rehearsal/performance period:* —

1st condition: low stress when the conductor was alone in an air-conditioned studio, thinking through the score and simulating his conducting gestures. Only minimal psycho-social stress occurred.
2nd condition: moderate stress when rehearsing the orchestra and later, during the final rehearsal in the concert hall. The cardio-vascular demands increased.
3rd condition: high stress when conducting the performance in public. Further increase in the cardio-vascular demands.

It seems that the physical work involved made only a trivial contribution to the 2nd and 3rd fold increments over the resting heart-rate as in condition 2, when even the starting heart rates were 30 beats higher than that of the peak attained in condition 1. The research team concluded that the elevated heart-rate created psycho-social stress augmented by the heat stress from the heavier clothing (his tail suit) which contributed to the highest rate of all. It was also evident that while the cardio-vascular load at the performance was considerable and sustained for more than 30 minutes and would have been experienced in similar situations on a fairly regular basis, it could be inferred that conducting is a good cardiac training exercise. The considered opinion therefore was that conducting an orchestra is a very stressful occupation, but for most conductors it is a desirable form of stress which subsides when the activity is completed. This may explain why, in part, conductors often live long lives and it may also be due to their love for, and dedication to, the profession, which is a well-established recipe for good health. Another important factor is the emotional satisfaction which musicians presumably gain from an intense appreciation of their art and associated sensory stimulations. I am sure, however, that the lives of musicians and conductors are not all beer and skittles but they are fortunate in having perhaps a nice balance between the good and the bad, the source of the good being music!'

Another health problem has been caused by the vast increase in the number of rehearsals and performances, which has resulted in hearing loss occurring earlier in life than was previously the case. When *Madama Butterfly* and *Turandot* are performed in the Sydney Opera House pit, some players have been able to plug their ears at the many brass climaxes while the unfortunate string players – with both hands occupied – cannot. In England, the Association of British Orchestras warned its players that under new European regulations, the playing of loud passages might become illegal and should this regulation ever be approved, many twentieth-century scores might have to be banned!

The Repetiteur–Coach

The designation 'repetiteur' stems from the many tasks that a pianist is expected to undertake, including playing *ad infinitum* a scaled-down version of the orchestral score while the production evolves, hence the title. Being a repetiteur provides the opportunity to learn about voice production, breath control and the relationship between text and music, so a good knowledge of the operatic languages – Italian, German, French and English – is necessary along with Russian and Czech; operas from those countries are now more frequently performed in the West than in the past.

Before ensemble and production rehearsals begin, most singers are glad of the opportunity to work with a good repetiteur who can sense a dormant interpretation and possibly suggest further ideas to the singer, especially with regard to the personality being portrayed. Such sessions become a two-way exploration with new ideas bounced back and forth. In this context, the best editions of Mozart's operas are useful as they include his very own stage directions, which indicate the specific vocal and dramatic colour he wanted. When ensemble rehearsals begin with the conductor in residence, problems sometimes arise if a repetiteur's conception of the music is obviously different to that of the conductor, or later still, the producer; but sensitive singers realize that every suggestion can be digested and melded into their composite portrayal of the rôle.

A repetiteur is not an accompanist but may be very good at being both. An accompanist plays the piano part exactly as the score indicates and follows the singer, while a repetiteur has to 're-compose' the orchestral score as piano reductions vary considerably from edition to edition in vocal scores. Keyboard facility is vital though not necessarily up to virtuoso standard but he or she must be able to read anything from one to eight vocal lines printed above the piano stave, to be aware of a particular singer's line, and to thoroughly know the orchestral score in order to simulate the different timbres of woodwind, strings and brass. Mozart's Finales are classic examples of orchestral writing that is well nigh impossible to play on the piano, so their basic harmonic structure has to be edited and played without any disruption to the tempo. During ensemble rehearsals, repetiteurs may be required to play or sing a missing voice part, but, like conductors, they are not always blessed with beautiful voices so it is not at all surprising that singers prefer to hear their cues played rather than sung! Being a repetiteur demands a unique talent beyond the capabilities of some first-class pianists and nothing is more infuriating for a conductor than a repetiteur who cannot follow every nuance and gesture.

‖: 47 :‖

During production rehearsals it is necessary for the conductor to be absent to work with the orchestra so the repetiteur assumes responsibility for the music if there is no assistant conductor. In this event, having to control a large cast of singers from the keyboard, especially if the repetiteur is seated some distance away, can be difficult. The reason for the unenviable position of the piano is to allow for a long line of staff consisting of the stage manager, assistant stage manager, language coach, producer, assistant producer, conductor and, frequently, understudies. When the production moves from the rehearsal room into the theatre, the repetiteur has to adapt quickly to the pit and the darkness, to not hearing the singers as before, and to seeing the conductor from a different angle.

Finally, when the orchestra arrives, the repetiteur often has a number of tasks including taking notes for the conductor, prompting, and conducting back-stage bands and choruses. Once the opera is in performance, some companies expect their music staff to take notes on how the cast is developing – or not as the case may be – and whether inaccuracies have become entrenched (a situation that demands further rehearsals). The repetiteur then begins all over again with the next assignment, which may be in a totally different style or language and complexity, not forgetting private practice in readiness for the next opera, which may be something of a pianistic challenge. It is of paramount importance, therefore, for any opera company to have an enthusiastic music staff who can work together as a team.

Vocal coaches are not usually members of an opera company although some are engaged on a guest contract basis. Their function is to coach special or uniquely difficult rôles, to develop musical and dramatic imagination, and to relieve the incredibly busy resident music staff. Vocal coaches are not ostensibly singing teachers and should never attempt to become involved in a singer's vocal technique (some do and sometimes better than the teacher) as this can set up confrontational problems for the singer and the teacher.

Nevertheless, coaches should obviously know a great deal about the art and craft of singing.

*C*horus Master

The Chorus Master has the unenviable position of working very hard for a considerable amount of time in training the chorus, and then the conductor may decide to change details in the interpretation; it is the conductor's privilege, but it can be frustrating. A sensitive Chorus Master will not only train, but enlarge the understanding of the whole opera, its composer and other aspects of the period in which the opera was written. Some prefer to play for their own rehearsals so as to shape their intentions rather than by talking or singing, especially if they have only a limited vocal accomplishment; other Chorus Masters need an accompanist.

The Chorus Master is always busy rehearsing and overseeing the chorus during production rehearsals, in case the producer places them in a difficult position or creates a vocal imbalance. The Chorus Master will conduct backstage during performances. Time also has to be found for regular auditions, as there is always a continual flow of singers joining and leaving the chorus. The Chorus Master (or an assistant) then has to rehearse the newcomers on their own so that they can join the main body on stage as soon as possible.

Arguably, the most awkward opera to rehearse is *Fidelio* because Beethoven's writing is notoriously un-vocal, especially for the sopranos and tenors. An astute Chorus Master will rehearse the final scene in a much lower key – even a fifth lower – so that the music is learnt with little strain. The pitch is then gradually raised as the rehearsals proceed; for a chorus in England the repetition allows for the unconscious absorption of German pronunciation by the whole chorus.

Chorus

Unlike a symphonic chorus, an opera chorus has to memorize the music, learn the vital cues that precede their entrances, be dramatically alert and responsive to the production, and need to know the complete score because they may only have a brief interjection in the middle of an ensemble. Some chorus parts are printed with the soprano, alto, tenor and bass lines in separate folders so that sopranos and mezzos are unaware of what the tenors and basses are singing, and vice versa; this makes the learning process much more difficult than when all the parts are printed together. In permanent companies the chorus works hard and long hours, with morning rehearsals and nightly performances for such vocally demanding operas as *Nabucco, Fidelio, Turandot* and *Die Meistersinger* – and sometimes even in the same season. On the other hand, operas in which they have little to do can be exhausting because they have to be in the theatre throughout the entire performance yet make only two short entrances, as for instance in Mozart's *Die Entführung aus dem Serail.*

In one world-famous opera house the union ruling was that male choristers had to make their entrances and exits on the same side of the stage as their dressing rooms, and likewise the female choristers. They then stood around on stage with little involvement in the drama going on all about them. Fortunately this attitude has disappeared, but such negativity can lead to "Greenroomitus" – a disease caused by sitting in the Green Room for long periods, gossiping and sniping at the principals. Usual comments are that they sing equally well, if not better than the principals, but are denied the opportunity; this is far from the truth as the music staff are always on the lookout for latent talent and naturally inform the management of any potential principal performers. Some choristers (relatively few) manage to make the transition to become principals in their own right and leave to work hard at their vocal improvement and find principal engagements elsewhere. Others quickly realize that they are not potential star material and, lacking the resilience for the grueling life of a soloist, prefer to remain conscientious choristers throughout their working lives. In non-permanent companies, however, the situation is quite different. Glyndebourne and Santa Fe, and similar companies, engage a new chorus each year from young, graduating singers some of whom are also given understudy positions and receive expert coaching. Being on stage with highly experienced singers in the same rôles is an invaluable asset as they can inwardly absorb, digest and integrate what they witness into their own personalities. In this way they are able to learn what it means to be a performer.

Orchestra

In 1780, Leopold Mozart wrote to his son, *'You should do your best to keep the whole orchestra in good humour; flatter them and cultivate all round attachment to yourself by judicious praise!'* Just over a hundred years later Richard Strauss wrote a similar injunction but from the player's perspective: *'and yet this malicious mob, the orchestra who plod their way in a weary mezzo forte, who refuse to play pp when accompanying imprecise chords in a recitative, unless the right man happens to be at the rostrum with what enthusiasm do they play tortured by these blunderers with no idea of rehearsing'.*

An orchestra is made up of any number of decidedly individual personalities in four instrumental groups – woodwind, brass, percussion and strings – each in its own guarded territory though united whenever tussles occur with whoever is on the rostrum. It is an explosive mix ignited by a conductor's mannerisms, idiosyncrasies and demands that easily become a regular nightmare for some well-seasoned players. There is no doubt that conductors need to have a great sense of psychology along with their other skills and crafts – even more so in opera orchestras – as the difficulties that crop up in the relationship are compounded by the unceasing repetition of the most popular operas. It is not surprising therefore that within the ranks of most orchestras lurk would-be conductors fully convinced that they could achieve much more than the current demagogue could.

Orchestral writing is as much involved in the dramatic situation as that acted out on stage. In *Così fan tutte* for instance, the throbbing strings simulate the passionate beating of Dorabella and Guiglielmo's hearts; in *Die Zauberflöte*, the instrumental hesitations and the silent bar describe Tamino's inability to express himself in the right words; the harmonic and rhythmic intensity of Don Giovanni's confrontation with the statue; and every bar in the Act 2 Finale of *Le nozze di Figaro* being just a few superb examples. Wagner built his music edifices on the *leitmotif* idea in counterpoint with the drama which was emulated later by Richard Strauss, though with a lighter touch. Verdi, Puccini, Massenet, Britten and many other composers all wrote magnificent orchestral music in their operas, so it is unfortunate when the drama emanating from the pit is often overlooked by an audience more intent on what is happening on stage.

Opera orchestras have expanded steadily over the centuries though when baroque operas are scheduled, the small, specialist ensembles required add a considerable expense to the budget while modern orchestras attempting to play in the 'old style' remain unconvincing. To be artistically (or politically) correct, those modern companies that engage specialist ensembles should raise their pits, construct genuine baroque sets entirely of wood, use candle-light and have the players don eighteenth-century wigs and costumes. If their intention is to put the clock back then they should also engage singers in their late teens and early twenties with voices to match, if Mozart's original Susanna, Barbarina, Don Giovanni and Donna Anna were anything to go by!

Up to Mozart's time orchestras were relatively small, as can be seen in a letter to his father during rehearsals for the première of *Idomeneo*. There were 6 violins at the first rehearsal and 12 at the second, a week later. Mozart must have been satisfied with the small number as there is no trace of any adverse comment but *Idomeneo* would never be performed today with so few, or with a week's gap between rehearsals. It is not always fully realized that in 1807 – two years after the première of *Fidelio* – the Vienna Philharmonic orchestra was made up of 55 musicians of which only 18 were fully professionals and the remainder, amateur!

During the last half of the eighteenth century, conductors slowly began to move from the harpsichord to stand in a central position in front of the orchestra. Players and their instruments in opera houses were only slightly below the level of the stage with the tall double-basses protruding and the continual up and down violin bows an irritating distraction, while the conductors towered over the whole proceedings. These visual obstacles lasted until larger theatres (the horseshoe style) and orchestra pits were constructed which was to directly influence the future course of music. In his *Grand traité d'in-strumentation et d'orchestration modernes*, Berlioz mentioned that the strings should be augmented, as they were practically inaudible, so that in the course of time, their numbers grew. The string sound was still barely audible in the theatre so the chin rest was invented which enabled players to firmly hold their instruments and produce a greater vibrato to enhance the sound. By the time that Wagner composed his mature operas, the string complement was 16 first violins, 16 seconds, 12 violas, 12 cellos and 8 double basses with the wind and brass sections increased accordingly.

Comparing the instrumentation in opera orchestras from Monteverdi to the present time clearly indicates the steady enlarge-ment mentioned above. Monteverdi's *L'incoronazione di Poppea* (1642) was written for a very small number of strings and various plucked continuo instruments with occasional recorder and trumpet parts. This admirably suited the relatively small palaces of the wealthy Italian families.

Mozart scored *Die Zauberflöte* (1791) for 2 flutes, 2 oboes, 2 clarinets, 2 bassoons, 2 horns, 2 trumpets, 3 trombones, timpani and strings with the exotic glockenspiel added to conjure up the scenes involving 'magic'. Incidentally, as no such instrument now exists, its actual sound cannot be clearly imagined although it must have been a keyboard rather than a mallet for the fast scale passages in Papageno's aria in Act 2. There have been various attempts to create an equivalent timbre using the celeste (too soft grained), or a xylophone (a wooden sound). A combination of both with a tinkling triangle for good measure has even been tried, but it proved to be unsatisfactory.

Beethoven's *Fidelio* (1805) was scored for the same size of orchestra (without the glockenspiel) but with a contra-bassoon for the dungeon scene, two additional horns (making four in all), and two (not the usual three) trombones. Numbers then stayed fairly constant until Meyerbeer and Berlioz experimented in their orchestration and Wagner reached his musical maturity. He expanded the wind section to 3 flutes and piccolo, 3 oboes and cor anglais, 3 clarinets and bass clarinet, 3 bassoons and contra-bassoon, 8 horns (4 of them also playing 'Wagner' tuba parts), 3 trumpets and bass trumpet, 4 trombones, contra-bass trombone and contra-bass tuba, 2 pairs of timpani, various percussion instruments and 6 harps with the number of strings as mentioned above. Richard Strauss continued with Wagner's style of orchestral polyphony, though with a much lighter texture and occasionally included bassett horns, which had not been used since Mozart's time.

Bernard Shaw described Verdi's writing for the orchestra as if it was for an 'oversized guitar', implying that it only provided an accompaniment but with little character of its own. Admirable as Bernard Shaw was as a knowledgeable music critic, his comment was a gross exaggeration. Verdi's early operas do have touches of the 'oversized guitar' but he included many subtle orchestral details in *Macbeth*, such as in the Witches' chorus, Lady Macbeth's arias, the subterranean band and in the chorus of Scottish refugees, which he was to echo in the Requiem. *La traviata*, *Rigoletto* and *Don Carlos* all have marvellous orchestral moments, while *Otello* (1887) and *Falstaff* (1893) are crammed full with highly imaginative strokes for the orchestra. They were written for triple woodwind and brass plus a bass trombone, timpani, percussion, harp (one only) and strings. Verdi sometimes wrote for the cimbasso, which was a bass instrument of the brass family but now obsolete, and he also preferred a bass trombone to the tuba. Puccini basically kept to Verdi's instrumentation with occasional exotic instruments for special effect, like the bells in *Tosca* (1900) and the off-stage oboe d'amore in *Madama Butterfly* (1904). Gounod, Bizet and Massenet all wrote for what had become the standard orchestra, but for the plaintive sound he wanted in *Werther* (1892), Massanet used a recently invented instrument, the saxophone.

Most twentieth-century opera composers kept to the instrumentation of Wagner, Verdi, Puccini and Richard Strauss with some exotic extras. A new type of opera orchestra was created when Britten composed his chamber operas for 13 soloists in which the flautist also plays the rare instrument, the bass flute – his chamber orchestra was a classic example of financial necessity being the mother of invention. Britten's younger contemporaries continued experimenting with the chamber ensemble, and more recently electronic instruments and synthesizers have also been incorporated.

Singers

With his inimitable wit, Rossini probably produced the ultimate tongue-in-cheek generalization about singers on whom, of course, he was dependent: '*How wonderful opera would be if there were no singers*'. Verdi, ever the perspicacious Italian patriot, adopted a more serious tone when he wrote, '*Germany has no lack of voices, they are almost more sonorous than Italian voices, but they consider the art of singing as a gymnastic exercise . . . Italian singers are often unjustifiably criticized for neglecting acting for the sake of bel canto yet how many are there who combine both, who can act and sing?'*

There is a misconception among the uninformed that opera singers are inevitably bad at acting, which may be true about some but is far too sweeping a generalization. Acting in opera is markedly different to acting in spoken drama for the simple reason that it is the conductor's timing of the music that governs the singer's movement and gesture throughout every performance, whereas in spoken drama the actor's timing stems from the producer's direction during the rehearsal period. That is not to deny that some opera singers indulge themselves in semaphore from which they can be weaned; likewise, the singers who plant themselves centre stage and sing directly to the audience while ignoring their upstage colleagues can be gently dissuaded.

During production rehearsals in spoken drama, actors tend to have the text literally in their hands, while singers have to memorize the complete score well before the first rehearsal; this is because they can then concentrate on the producer while simultaneously being aware of the conductor and the sound of the repetiteur's piano. The vast majority of operas have vocal ensembles ranging from duets to nonets and beyond, with each participant singing a different text with a different emotional response. If this happened in a play by Ibsen or Shaw, all bedlam would break out unless the playwright's intention was a heated argument! It should also be understood that opera houses are usually larger than drama theatres so a singer's facial expressions have to be larger than life to register at the back of the auditorium.

Unlike any other performer such as a pianist, clarinetist or violinist, the singer has an internal instrument that can be influenced by health, mood, climate, weather or air-conditioning. The voice depends on deep-seated breathing to support the vocal cords, which are contained in the larynx, and connected to the mouth and nose via the lungs and windpipe. Although singers and woodwind players breathe similarly, the singer's resonating chambers (the equivalent of the belly of a stringed instrument) are in the head, face and chest cavities and, with the hard and soft palates, create the tone which colours the singer's entire vocal personality. Flutes, clarinets, violins and cellos all have fairly standard measurements but the voice is dependent on the length of the vocal cords – and which vary between 17–25 millimetres for male, and 12–17 millimetres for female singers. After puberty, the length of the vocal cord remains the same for females but it may change as a boy matures, causing the phenomena of the voice 'breaking'.

Every voice has three registers – top, middle and bottom – and if the transition from one to another is not properly mastered, deterioration can occur and often rapidly. This is usually caused by the *passagio* (passage or bridge) between the middle and head registers not having been properly negotiated, with the upper notes becoming flat in both pitch and colour. The physical sensation of singing is felt in all the registers, but being an instinctive craft, young singers often tie themselves up in psychological knots if they are made too much aware of the physiology. A more constructive approach is for the teacher to employ pictorial images as a spur to the pupil's imagination so that the vocal technique is well planted in the subconscious, and it then becomes instinctive.

There is a tendency to ridicule singers for their supposed lack of musicianship but the art as well as the craft develops from different physical and emotional impulses to those of an instrumentalist. The latter usually begins to study music at an early age but a singer may only discover that he or she has any sort of voice around puberty but lacks practice in musicianship and performing. This, in some ways, is actually an advantage, for those singers who read music easily often overwork their instruments, forgetting that vocal cords have their own 'memory', which needs time to settle into the subconscious. Nevertheless it is essential for singers to learn to play the piano, not necessarily to a high standard but sufficient to learn the correct notes and rhythms. A laborious process perhaps, but the fingers help the process of memorizing, and, in the long term, so much more personally satisfying than copying a singer on a recording. Ill-advised singers learn arias and even whole rôles in this way but it is foolhardy as the recording may contain inaccuracies while the unique timbre of the singer on the disc should never be imitated, otherwise an individual vocal personality will never develop. At one time young singers gained valuable experience by singing with a choir or amateur operatic society whose standards were variable perhaps, but would benefit from performing opportunities and discovering the need for self-discipline.

Another factor that instrumentalists should consider when criticizing singers is the very nature of their different crafts. Orchestral players regularly perform Beethoven's symphonies with the music in front of them, they are seated with adequate lighting and contact with the conductor at all times. Singers, on the other hand, have to master many more skills: shape words consisting of vowels and consonants in the same time frame as an instrumental phrase; memorize a number of lengthy rôles and usually in a foreign language; understand the dramatic implications of the production; follow a conductor some distance away or perhaps masked by the set or other singers; be blinded by stage lighting and, in the course of a single act, have to change costume a number of times. Finally their workload may include a number of rôles with one in performance, another in rehearsal, and a third at coaching stage. With so much involved it is not surprising that singers are not always perfect in every one of these skills, however determined they may be. Conversely, string players can learn a great deal from singers about good breathing which results in quality musical phrasing.

Some English-speaking singers are reluctant to sing in their own language and are lazy about enunciation. Their feeble excuse usually is that English is not a good language for singing because of its many consonants and diphthongs – yet Shakespeare managed to revel in its vast, colourful vocabulary! Thanks to Vaughan Williams, Britten and other masters at setting the English language, that rather blinkered attitude is now disappearing, but, even if not perfect as conversational linguists, singers should also be able to perform in Italian, German and French, with Russian and Czech for good measure. To pronounce and enunciate any language properly, every word has to be embedded in the singer's subconscious, but when a rôle has to be re-learnt in a different language, the whole process begins again. It is not merely a matter of learning a new text because the whole physical and mental placing is different in each language. Paradoxically, although original language texts never need updating apart from one or two outdated speech idioms, translations need revising every generation. And even today some singers repeat nonsensical Victorian translations in which the rhyme was paramount, and 'thee' and 'thou' used unsparingly.

There is a rampant belief among young singers that enunciation in Italian is easy because the consonants are soft and final consonants are very few, yet when Italian singers perform *secco recitative* – however fast – their enunciation is exemplary. In German the final consonants are vital to understand grammar and tense so that regardless of language, poor enunciation should never be condoned. French also requires careful study as English-speaking singers often labour under the misapprehension that it is sung in the nose, which is far from the truth for the vowels are as pure as their Italian counterparts. Russian is more of a problem in that the look of the word on the page bears no relation to the Western alphabet so the formation of the sound is difficult to visualize and, without prior knowledge of the language, Russian rôles have to be learnt by rote.

Another difficult skill to master is *secco recitative*. The adjective, *secco* (dry), implies a recitative with keyboard rather than orchestra; as *recitative* literally means 'recite', a *secco recitative* is therefore intended to propel the action between the arias and ensembles which requires parlando (speaking) on the notes rather than singing them. There also has to be the realization that – having the freedom to vary the tempo for dramatic purposes – it should not be confused with the printed long and short note values which composers such as Mozart provided for emphasis and inflection; this subtlety is often misunderstood or completely ignored.

'Marking' is a technique used in production rehearsals to save the vocal cords as only half the normal tone and volume is brought into play. Some singers find marking very difficult to do and sing the vocal line an octave (or two) lower; either way the vocal balance is distorted, especially in ensembles, which only irritates conductors. They become even more anxious when singers persist in marking throughout the production rehearsal period as it supposes a possible camouflage of the singer's vocal shortcomings which only become apparent when it is too late to rectify.

Singers can benefit enormously from listening intently to the various instrumental colours in the orchestra. Sensitive artists can use oboes, clarinets, bassoons, trumpets and strings to conjure up different dramatic situations for dramatic purposes. Singers new to working with an orchestra also discover that the orchestra gives them a much greater vocal support than the piano, whose sound starts to die as soon as the notes are struck; the orchestra is as if it were a well-sprung mattress that supports the voice. There are some singers who imagine that the orchestra's *raison d'être* is merely to be their accompanist but they quickly learn to follow the conductor rather than lead, or their performance may be ruined by the conductor coming off a pause on a well-sung top note before the singer is ready, or alternatively conducting the aria at an impossible tempo. Being beholden to the conductor, singers should realize that an amicable working relationship needs to be established or a battle of wits will ensue with the singer the inevitable loser. This is simply because no conductor is prepared to lose his or her authority in front of the orchestra. If, on the other hand, the conductor follows the singer as a sympathetic accompanist, their performance will suffer from a lack of momentum; singers usually expect a firm but gentle hand even when they say the opposite! '*Old maestri teach the young singers, and the old singers teach the young maestri*' is an old adage now largely forgotten but the experience of a lifetime ought to pass on from one generation to another.

Worldwide opera administrations now have instantaneous contact with their counterparts and are immediately aware of any promising singers on the horizon. As a result, careers can now be launched nationally and/or internationally more rapidly than ever before. This advantageous situation also has a disadvantage for, when a talented singer 'arrives' too early, his or her vocal ability and personality can be over-stretched and a promising career over before it has hardly begun. Modern air travel also presents problems for a singer – especially if just starting out – because it is only natural to accept tempting offers and, as a result, succumb to physical and mental fatigue. Previous generations of singers were compelled to travel by sea, which was beneficial in that it provided some time to rest and indulge in further study. Because of the speed by which a career can now be launched, it is worthwhile to obtain the services and advice of a good Artist's Manager before accepting too many engagements, as many performances are now cancelled as a direct result of physical and vocal fatigue. Although substitute singers can be flown in quickly between Europe and America, it is much more difficult between the Northern Hemisphere and Australia because of the immense distance and jet lag involved.

Before the era of *Bel Canto*, operatic voices must have been considerably lighter in texture than today as singers were far younger, one example being Mozart's original Barbarina who was only twelve years old at the time, and who sang Susanna when she was only seventeen. Mozart's first Sarastro was not much older, his Don Giovanni only twenty-two, and Donna Anna twenty-four; singers at those ages today, however talented, would not be acceptable by either opera managements or audiences. Even in 1805, when Beethoven's *Fidelio* was first performed, both his Florestan and Leonore were under twenty. So much more is demanded from singers now than would have ever been countenanced previously, not only in voice but also in physical prowess and agility on stage – such as hand-stands, cartwheels when making an entrance, singing while flat on the back or strapped in a harness flying above the stage as gods or goddesses. One extreme case was for an open-air performance of *Die Zauberflöte*; the Queen of the Night had to sing both her arias suspended above the stage in an electrical engineer's maintenance box. Fireworks exploded all around and her only contact with the conductor was by a television monitor with very little sound relayed from the orchestra. In the past it was believed that such antics would hinder vocal support and breath control, although it was probably due to Prima Donnas firmly dictating what they would or would not do. Almost any physical contortion an actor can accomplish is also possible for a singer, except anything that hinders deep-seated breathing for the singing voice has to be projected out over the orchestra rather than upstage. When a voice is directed upstage, it disappears into the wings, but if it is aimed even slightly in front of the proscenium arch, it will project into the auditorium.

The media perpetually promotes the exaggerated myth of a singer's 'temperament' which is simply a synonym for bad manners. Nerves must always play an important part in a performer's make-up as without them they appear cold or aloof, but conversely, being over-nervous creates havoc with the control of the voice and intonation is affected – sharpness in particular. Uncontrolled nerves can also cause a voice to crack but nerves never disappear altogether and sometimes even increase with a successful career. Vocal control is an imperative for the obvious reason that if Mimi was really to cry in Act 4 of *La bohème*, the soprano's vocal cords would be affected by her tears; similarly, if Adele genuinely laughed in her 'Laughing Song' in *Die Fledermaus!* Performers should bear in mind William Wordsworth's 1807 letter to Lady Beaumont in which he wrote that poetry is *'emotion recollected in tranquillity'*; likewise opera singers technically need to simulate the emotions of the characters they portray – emotions that they have previously felt intensely, and digested.

There are a number of ways by which singers prepare themselves for a performance. Some sing through the whole rôle with full voice in the morning of the performance while others do not sing one note or open their mouth even to speak in order to 'save' it for the evening. Appetites are also affected, with some believing that eating a hearty meal (and/or its sexual equivalent) a few hours before will enhance their performance while others abstain till afterwards by way of relaxation. With the intense competition from glamorous film and television stars, outsize singers today have to make a much greater effort to lose weight than ever before even though their tonal beauty may suffer, but a gargantuan girth is no longer acceptable; that is unless he or she is such an exceptional artist that their bulk becomes irrelevant.

Some singers are like empty vessels into which an interpretation has to be poured by a coach or a repetiteur, while others are totally independent, preferring to develop their own conception of a rôle. Others possess superb voices but are not so good at dramatic expression; some are excellent at acting yet have only moderately good voices; those who excel at both, however, warrant the title, artist. This not only encompasses vocal interpretation, physique and charisma, but is also apparent in ways often overlooked by the audience. One such artist performing the Countess in Strauss's *Capriccio* mastered the footwork required to change the strings of the harp for different keys, and although the real harp was played in the orchestra pit, she made the correct pedal changes with her feet!

At the apex of the category of singers and artists are the Divas and Prima Donnas. Diva is the Italian superlative for goddess, while Prima Donna is literally the first soprano in an ensemble; if there are two sopranos, then the second is designated Seconda Donna although the term Prima Donna has come to mean more than simply the one who sings the highest line. At the very top, however, is La Stupenda, but that title has been conferred by universal consent only once in modern times. During the *bel canto* era, the realm of opera expanded so that Diva and Prima Donna reigned supreme and both became subjects for criticism. Berlioz wrote, *'I loathe Divas, they are the curse of true music and musicians'.* Monsieur Croche (Debussy) went even further with: *'You are quite right to prefer dogs, they are more entertaining than concert artists and cows, more prepossessing than great prima donnas.'* It is strange that male artists were never granted an equivalent status.

The title Diva has now become fashionable because Prima Donna has come to imply a singer who indulges in tantrums and fights her colleagues, whereas a Diva refuses to descend to such mundane behaviour. Whether Diva or Prima Donna, they are sometimes seduced by their own charisma so a useful ploy on the morning of a performance if the Prima Donna professes to be unwell is to inform her that the understudy is very talented and ready to take her place. For some mysterious reason the Prima Donna's illness vanishes as quickly as it arrived! It is extremely rare to have two Prima Donnas in the same opera and a mezzo-soprano Prima Donna is rarer still. Berlioz, in the Sixth Evening of his *Les Soirées de l'orchestre*, satirized the operatic pecking order in an imaginary company with a scale of fees based on the cost of each syllable! A fictitious fee structure could be constructed today as *Che* ($1), *gelida* ($3), *manina* ($3), *se* ($1), *la* ($1), *laschia* ($2), *riscaldar* ($3) – a grand total of $14 for Puccini's one phrase. Multiply the cost for four major stars for each performance in an opera season and the result would be an astronomical sum! Nevertheless, the fees paid to top opera singers come nowhere near those paid to sports idols.

When a young and eager singer accepts an engagement and fails to make an impression, the Management soon forgets that it was at their invitation in the first place! On the other hand, one of the most difficult tasks for a General Manager is to inform a singer that his or her career is rapidly nearing its end and the rôles in which they had been highly acclaimed by both the public and the press are no longer possible. Some singers deny this fact of life, but astute ones retire gracefully while others indulge in many Farewell Performances. In the Sixth Evening of his *Les Soirées de l'orchestre*, Berlioz devotes one chapter to the life-cycle of a successful tenor which aspiring singers might do well to read; his biting satire is still relevant today and will, no doubt, remain so.

As their careers wane, there are two worthwhile options available for those who still want to be involved with singing one way or another: to accept minor rôles or establish a teaching practice, although successful singers do not always make good teachers whereas mediocre singers are sometimes excellent teachers. It is ironic that those singers who devote their whole careers to performing the comprimario roles are, in some ways, more fortunate than their more illustrious colleagues. This is mainly due to the character rôles in which they have specialized usually being vocally less demanding so that the voice withstands the inevitable wear and tear much better. When the Communist regimes collapsed in Russia and Eastern Europe, contingents of first-rate singers were suddenly available in the West and were soon snapped up. This injection was beneficial but the unexpectedly large pool of singers on which to draw appeared to cause some established careers in the West to be truncated; that predicament reiterates the time-honoured adage that a performer is only as good as his or her most recent performance!

After being accepted into a company at the chorus and/or understudy level, ambitious singers are gradually offered more and more tempting rôles — a moment when a young singer needs to take stock of his or her position in the company hierarchy. Being a resident artist with a secure contract and attractive prospects can be gratifying but that very security is a two-edged sword. Complacency is the death knell for any artist so if the singer has gone as far as possible within the company, an artist with ambition should seek advancement elsewhere, even if it means having to take a step backwards for a while.

There is really no such thing as a 'small part' for a minor rôle is as difficult to perform as a full-length rôle because the whole opera has to be learnt and understood in order to contribute a rounded character in, perhaps, a few bars of one or two phrases. Bruno Walter has been quoted as asking who would be singing the second prisoner in Beethoven's *Fidelio*, which he was to conduct. When he was asked why he needed to know that rather than who would sing Leonore and Florestan, his reply was that if the second prisoner was well chosen, then all the other rôles would undoubtedly have been as carefully cast!

Despite the age-old question of where do the most beautiful voices originate it is impossible to generalize. Although many countries have evolved their unique vocal timbres, there are physiological differences, due to the shape and thickness of the hard palate, which varies between continents and racial characteristics. Italian tenors, for instance, sound quite different from their German, English, Irish or Scandinavian counterparts. Russia has produced many more deep basses than any other country, while Anglo-Saxon countries tend to produce singers with a wider musical and intellectual background than elsewhere. There is also a myth that more singers emerge from Wales and Australia than from anywhere else, and certainly their relatively small populations have produced many good singers, perhaps because of the Welsh open vowel sounds and by Australia's sun loving — and, to a certain extent – less inhibited culture than other Western countries. One internationally famous accompanist, who was born and bred in Australia, humorously suggested that the reason why Australia had produced so many singers was because they have to squint in the intense sun. The squint causes the frontal cheek muscles to lift and allows the resonating chambers in the mask of the face to function all the time!

The Fach System

A character is reflected in the singer's tessitura and timbre so that high and light sopranos suggest innocence while lower voices suggest maturity and greater dramatic power, but there is some overlapping. Monteverdi composed the rôle of Penelope for a mezzo-soprano in his *Il ritorno d'Ulisse in patria* to highlight the plight of a woman 'more sinned against than sinning'; the soprano timbre would not have been so telling. Rossini's Rosina in *Il barbiere di Siviglia* is also a mezzo-soprano although she is sometimes sung by a soprano, and as a result, Rosina becomes a different personality. Another exception is Violetta in *La traviata*, who can be interpreted by a light soprano suiting her frailty, by a lyric soprano who is able to bring out her warmth and passion, or by a spinto soprano, who can portray Violetta's innate nobility and dignity. This spectrum of vocal colour allied to tessitura and personality is known internationally by the German word *fach* (compartment) and categorized as follows:

Coloratura Soprano Having a very high tessitura and able to perform florid music. Examples are The Queen of the Night in *Die Zauberflöte*, Zerbinetta in *Ariadne auf Naxos* and Olympia in *Les Contes d'Hoffmann*.

Lyric Soprano A voice with a finer grain and a greater cantabile line than a coloratura or a dramatic soprano. There are many examples including Ilia in *Idomeneo*, Mimi in *La bohème* and Liù in *Turandot*.

Dramatic Soprano One who expresses highly charged emotions with a wide range of dynamics and is able to soar over large vocal and orchestral ensembles. Leonore in *Fidelio*, Norma in Bellini's opera of the same name and Verdi's Lady Macbeth are just three examples.

Soubrette This vocal category has now virtually disappeared but it used to signify a high, light soprano, often physically and vocally on the small side and specializing in coquettish and vivacious characters, usually maidservants. Examples include Mozart's Susanna, Zerlina, Blonde and Despina, all of whom are now portrayed much more naturally and with a greater vocabulary of expression. Incidentally, mezzo-sopranos are now also cast as Despina because the mezzo-soprano timbre vividly suggests her earthiness.

Spinto The Italian word for 'pushed' or 'urged on'. The vocal range is similar to that of the lyric soprano but with greater power and a firmer legato line, especially in the lower register. Examples are Leonora in *Il trovatore*, the title rôles in *Tosca*, *Aida*, the Countess in *Figaro* and even some Wagnerian rôles.

Mezzo-Soprano Italian for 'middle soprano' meaning halfway between soprano and contralto with either dramatic or lyrical potential, or both. Like the dramatic soprano, the voice is ideally suited to the dark and dramatic rôles such as Amneris in *Aida*, Azucena in *Il Trovatore* and Wagner's *Fricka*. A different kind of mezzo-soprano is required for Cherubino in *Figaro* and Der Komponist in *Ariadne auf Naxos*, though both characters can be performed by lyric or even spinto sopranos.

Contralto The Italian fusion of two syllables, *contra* and *alto*, implying the opposite to high. The designation originated during the period when polyphonic church music predominated and the vocal part above the tenor line was called 'haute' (high). 'Haute' gradually became 'haute-contre', and finally contra-alto; consequently it is the lowest female voice. True contraltos have become exceedingly rare so that their rôles are now, more often than not, sung by mezzo-sopranos. Examples are Arnalta (*L'incoranazione di Poppea*), Mistress Quickly (*Falstaff*) and Delilah (*Samson et Dalila*), though tenors sometimes sing the other contralto rôles of the Witch in *Hansel und Gretel* and Orlofsky in *Die Fledermaus*.

Lyric Tenor The male equivalent of a lyric soprano. Many examples can be cited including Rudolfo (*La bohème*), Alfredo (*La traviata*), Nemorino (*L'elisir d'amore*) and Fenton (*Falstaff*).

Tenor Leggiero Comparable to a lyric tenor but also sings more florid music especially in the middle and upper registers. Typical rôles include Almaviva (*Il barbiere di Siviglia*), Don Ottavio (*Don Giovanni*) and Ernesto (*Don Pasquale*).

Counter-Tenor Or contre-tenor, meaning the voice that sang either above, or below, the tenor line in polyphonic church music. The voice is developed from the bass and baritone head voice (falsetto), but there still is controversy about its production and sometimes it is referred to as male alto. Baroque opera includes many examples but more recently Benjamin Britten exploited the timbre in *Midsummer Night's Dream*, *Death in Venice* and in a number of his other works.

Tenore Robusto A designation rarely used today but was once a tenor with a markedly full and vigorous (robust) delivery. It was similar to the Wagnerian helden tenor with examples including such rôles as the Calaf (*Turandot*), Florestan (*Fidelio*), Radames (*Aida*) and Peter Grimes, although the latter was composed for a much lighter voice.

Helden Tenor German for a 'heroic' tenor – a voice with stamina, power and clarity yet having a lyrical quality. The title came into existence with Wagner's music dramas although he fully intended that Lohengrin should be sung by a tenor versed in Bellini's *bel canto* idiom, a fact often overlooked! Other helden tenor roles include Max (*Der Freischütz*), Tristan (*Tristan und Isolde*) and Bacchus (*Ariadne auf Naxos*).

Comprimario Tenor One who performs the subsidiary rôles (usually comic) that do not require first-class voices. Examples are Pedrillo (*Die Entführung aus dem Serail*), Basilio (*Figaro*), Monostatos (*Die Zauberflöte*), Spallanzani (*Les Contes d'Hoffmann*) and many others. Pedrillo however has a quite difficult aria for most comprimario tenors to sing.

High Baritone A baritone with a very secure top register though the lower register must still have resonance. Examples include Tonio (*Pagliacci*), Count di Luna (*Il trovatore*), and the title rôles in *Don Giovanni* and *Le nozze di Figaro*.

Baritone A baritone with an even delivery throughout the registers. Examples cover a vast repertoire, including Papageno, Guglielmo, Don Giovanni, Silvio (*Pagliacci*), Germont (*La traviata*) and Sid (*Albert Herring*).

Baritone Martin A uniquely French voice with the vocal characteristics of both a tenor and a baritone. The rôle of Pelleas in Debussy's opera is the most famous example but there are many others in the French repertoire.

Basso Profundo The deepest bass voice capable of expressing solemn and profound moments although not always vocally flexible. Examples include Sarastro (*Die Zauberflöte*), King Philip (*Don Carlos*), Gremin (*Eugene Onegin*), the title rôle in *Boris Godunov* and King Fisher in *The Midsummer Marriage*.

Basso Cantante A bass specializing in lyrical rôles such as

Colline (*La bohème*), Don Giovanni, Sarastro and even Boris Godunov. In German opera, the basso cantante with a darker timbre admirably suits Wotan and Hans Sachs.

Basso Buffo A bass specializing in comic rôles such as Leporello, Dulcamara and Gianni Schicci to name just a few. Mozart's operatic ensembles now often require the two lowest male voices to interchange their parts because his writing took into account the original singer's tessitura, which is sometimes awkward today.

In Germany during the early years of the nineteenth century, artists were expected to perform both plays and opera and to be more skilled at acting than singing. As a result, the rôle of Florestan was given to a comic actor with a high, firm singing voice while Pizarro was described by one commentator as *'an insignificant singer, a poor musician but a zealous actor'*. Audiences today would never accept actors in these and other major rôles in opera.

Understudies

Understudies were not thought to be necessary until recently, but with the hectic life involved in opera today they have become important, even though some companies still take the risk doing without. In many companies, understudies are expected to fend for themselves without any rehearsal (the accepted norm in most parts of Europe). Some spend their entire careers as understudies without a single opportunity in which to prove themselves. Others begin their careers as understudies and through hard work, determination and never missing an opportunity, mature into performers in their own right.

Those companies that do engage complete understudy casts provide intensive music and production rehearsals to benefit the whole world of opera as proven by the many singers who began their careers as understudies at Santa Fe and Glyndebourne. In the 1960s the Glyndebourne Festival decided to take the system a stage further. The Touring Company was created so that young singers and conductors would have a chance to develop after the Festival came to an end each summer. The opera-going public around England also benefited, for they could experience the full Glyndebourne productions without the cost of travelling to Sussex, or expensive tickets.

P*rompter*

Prompting for spoken drama is totally different to prompting for opera. In the former, the prompter is in the wings and prompts only when an actor 'dries', that is, forgets the lines. For opera, the prompter sits in a small box in the centre of the stage and mouths or whispers every word or line *before* it is sung; even for such exclamations as the *Ha, ha* for the fairies in the last act of Verdi's *Falstaff*. Being in such a confined position for a lengthy opera can cause terrible back problems or a perpetual stoop, which Richard Strauss affectionately caricatured with Monsieur Toupe in *Capriccio*. Strauss composed the scene in 5/4 time to mirror the prompter's bewilderment and awkwardness at being let out of his box like the prisoners coming up for air during Act I of Beethoven's *Fidelio*!

A prompt box seems to be more necessary for Italian than German opera singers, probably because the Italian *bel canto* repertoire has so many exclamations like 'Ciel, Dei, Pieta, Numi'. Their inter-changeability can be very confusing in the heat of the moment and can easily cause a singer to jump to a totally different sentence, phrase or even another opera, as has happened on more than one occasion. Another factor may be the difference between the intrinsic Italian and German character; the former being emotionally instinctive and the latter more intellectually orientated.

Music Library

A company music library is vital for valuable rehearsal time can be lost for any number of reasons during a rehearsal: when the conductor has to search for a recognizable starting point for the orchestra and is unable to find one; in some editions, the orchestral parts have bar numbers while the conductor's score has rehearsal letters or even worse, neither. The librarian has to prepare the vocal scores, which can be as many as thirty for any one opera and all the orchestral material, keeping everything in good condition with accurate markings, cuts and alterations all clearly marked. The conductor, the singers and the orchestra are then spared unnecessary anxiety but a tussle can easily develop between a conductor and a player over a particular phrase, time wasted and nerves stretched only to discover that the score and parts are radically different. Another tedious chore is the erasing of previous gratuitous graffiti, correcting long-standing printed errors and repairing tattered parts; nothing is more exasperating for any musician than having to work from such material.

Study and Beyond
Conductor Training

Conducting is the most complicated craft of all, yet there is a prevailing belief that it is unteachable. Or as one eminent maestro has stated, it can be learnt in five minutes! Another misapprehension is that whereas instrumentalists have an instrument on which to practice, conductors need an orchestra at their beck and call, which is, of course, financially prohibitive. The craft of conducting is as teachable as any other artistic discipline which develops from an innate talent, ambition and personality. But as it involves other performers – ranging from just a handful to a hundred or more – an aspiring conductor needs first to be in command of his or her own inner resources. This includes intense concentration allied to lateral thinking, for the conductor needs to observe his or her own actions and reactions in rehearsal and, at the same time, make split-second decisions regarding the sound emanating from the orchestra; whether to stop because of a mistake or to continue in the hope that the error will not recur. Self-discipline is so important that a legend evolved about one eminent conductor who, prior to going on stage for a performance, always sat with a potted geranium in front of him and concentrated so hard that the geranium would begin to wilt – a signal that he was ready to conduct the performance!

Musicians are fully aware of the need for an accurate ear, but not every conductor is aurally equipped by nature. Thus before conducting studies begin, this faculty may have to be developed and exercised. Another prerequisite is a thorough knowledge of composition embracing harmony, counterpoint, figured bass and orchestration, which will provide an awareness of the many different musical styles during the past three to four hundred years. Having keyboard ability is also very useful as, apart from studying a score at the piano, it will later stand the aspiring conductor in good stead by serving a valuable apprenticeship as a repetiteur.

Conductors who intend to work in opera need to have a knowledge of the major operatic languages – Italian, German, French, English – and to understand the operas of Tchaikovsky and Janáček which are now in the repertoire of most opera houses in the West. Bruno Walter, who was a very good pianist, believed that participating in chamber music was important as it not only provides an abundance of fine music, but it encourages a sense of ensemble and promotes collaboration with other musicians. He was also convinced that to be a complete human being and, ergo, a better conductor, all the fine arts and philosophy are just as important – an aspect that some conductors today tend to overlook.

It is well known that Lully died from gangrene as a result of hitting his foot with his enormous mace with which he kept the orchestra in time. This unfortunate circumstance led to the use of the less life-threatening violin bow and a nod of the continuo player's head, but the first use of a baton is attributed to Louis Spohr when he rehearsed in London: *'I produced my baton from my pocket and gave the signal to begin. The novelty aroused their attention and, helped by seeing the time beaten out clearly, the players performed with a spirit and correctness unknown previously. The baton triumphed and no conductor was seen again at the piano in an orchestral work.'* Whether a baton is used or not is a matter of personal preference as some conductors achieve marvellous results without; for them the baton is inanimate and impersonal. Due to modern mass production they are often made from fibreglass, in standardized lengths and weight, and are eminently practical, as they are unbreakable. They are lethal, however, when they shred and get under the conductor's skin (causing excruciating pain) or fly out of the hand to harpoon a player.

When conducting, the left and right arms should be as independent as possible for perpetual duplication only diminishes the conductor's palate of expressive gestures. The eyes are equally important in communicating a conductor's intentions and musical character so a full-length mirror is very useful, as it becomes an alter ego to reflect the external reality as opposed to what is internally imagined. Also, to establish a real sense of clarity in the nebulous working area in front of a conductor, simple exercises can be practiced in front of the mirror to define the complete range of dynamics from *ppp* to *ffff*. Nothing is more irritating to an orchestra than a conductor who gesticulates frantically and, at the same time shouts, *'why aren't you playing piano'*! In operatic conducting, each hand can be used for a specific purpose apart from controlling the overall flow of the music; the right hand (or baton) indicates tempo and rhythm for the orchestra while the left hand cues the singers. If, instead, the right hand was used for the singers, the players might easily interpret the gesture as an *accelerando*, creating havoc all round!

After thoroughly studying the craft of conducting, enrolling as a student in an opera school is an excellent way of gaining experience and making mistakes (learning constructively from them) out of the limelight. Conducting production classes of operatic scenes with piano accompaniment is also invaluable in learning something of the vast repertoire, and, at the same time consolidating the gestures previously studied in front of a mirror but now exercised with live performers. Opera schools also mount fully staged productions enabling a student conductor to work alongside an experienced maestro and to take over a performance or two in preparation for a similar situation in the future.

*O*peratic Training for Singers

Dramatic training for singers — as distinct from vocal tuition — only really began during the twentieth century. Before that time, opera production was minimal by modern standards, with the composer rather than a producer directing rehearsals for the first performance and a stage manager supervising any revivals. Then, as the need for producers became apparent, with productions becoming more sophisticated, a greater dramatic aptitude was expected from performers and thorough operatic training was obviously necessary.

There are now many opera schools all over the Western world catering for the vast numbers of young singers coming forward every year. Most university music departments include opera in their course structure, usually as an academic subject; many try to mount one or occasionally two annual productions as an extramural activity. Conservatoria and music colleges provide more comprehensive courses but their cost in comparison with instrumental studies tends to influence the opera budget. Enrolment in an opera school should only be considered after the voice itself has been well and truly established and musicianship well under way, and should therefore come under the heading of postgraduate study. As a result, fewer students are enrolled and there is the perennial problem of more female than male singers, mainly because male voices mature much later. In the smaller opera schools, this imbalance usually means that Puccini's *Suor Angelica* (entirely female), Vaughan Williams's *Riders to the Sea* and Poulenc's *The Carmelites* (both with few male singers), are regularly performed as the year's major production. Those schools having sufficient numbers of tenors and baritones tend to choose a Mozart opera – an excellent choice to encourage vocal and mental discipline, good ensemble singing and to engender poise and elegance with which few students would have previously been familiar.

Mozart's rôles require considerable vocal accomplishment and concentration over long periods as even with cuts any one of his major operas takes approximately three hours. Britten's *Albert Herring* is also useful as it has many of the skills required by Mozart without too many of his vocal hurdles. And performing Britten enables young singers to experience twentieth-century harmonies, irregular rhythms and phrase lengths. Scenes from Verdi, Puccini and Richard Strauss are all performed by opera schools at least under workshop conditions, while Beethoven's *Fidelio*, Debussy's *Pelléas et Mélisande* and Rossini's *Guillaume Tell* have all been successful in full presentations. Obvious comparisons with famous stars are too often made, of course, while the memory of their own youthful vocal inadequacies may haunt students for the remainder of their careers.

A major study in any opera school should be *secco recitative*, for any young singer having only just learnt how to 'place' the singing voice has then to 'speak' on pitch (parlando) which can easily create confusion. Performing *secco recitative* also involves the use of the appoggiatura, which is used to fill in the interval (usually a third) between two notes. Composers at one time rarely wrote appoggiaturas into their scores, but executants from the baroque period right up to Rossini and Donizetti were expected to know when and how to use them. A bone of contention in many opera schools is whether students should sing in the original language or their own, but there are valid reasons for both. The original language allows for close contact with the composer's setting — assuming that the student has an understanding of the language and its pronunciation — and the inflection of every word. In the language of the singer, however, the intensity of verbal expression springs directly from the subconscious and is more instinctive even if it is spoken and sung badly.

A problem that opera schools face is the availability of an orchestra. It is imperative to have as many opportunities as possible to sing with an orchestra as there are a number of important differences to singing with piano. The instrumental faculty of a Conservatorium or college has to focus on the symphonic repertoire, and will often have only a limited time to devote to orchestral rehearsals on top of its academic and concerto studies; meanwhile opera requires far more orchestral rehearsal time and operatic writing is quite different to that of the symphonic repertoire. The paradox is that young instrumentalists can benefit from the experience of opera, as, of the vast numbers of graduating instrumental students, only a few actually go on to make solo careers. The majority hopefully find their way into symphony and opera orchestras, and usually with only a basic knowledge of the repertoire for either.

A comprehensive opera school develops a rounded performer with Movement and Dance which provides a sense of physical involvement and body rhythm. The Gavotte, Menuet, Polka, Mazurka, Polonaise and the Viennese Waltz all occur in opera and need practicing to the point where they become second nature. In fact the whole gamut of stagecraft covering basic make-up, exotic hand gestures (as for *Madama Butterfly*), dying gracefully, handling crinolines and fans, finding a chair while walking backwards, and for male students, fencing, all have to be thoroughly exercised as there is now no room in the profession for clumsy singers. Despite all the above, star pupils frequently fail to achieve success in the profession while more reticent students forge ahead. It is not so unusual for a young male singer to boast that he is a 'Verdi baritone' long before he has even found the full measure of his vocal talent. With so much involved in arriving at so-called 'stardom' it is not surprising that there is an extensive fall-out after the termination of official studies.

Singing Teachers

Opera schools concentrate on the dramatic skills and stage-craft so vocal training is a quite separate discipline, but finding the right teacher can take a long time. Some singers prefer to work with a teacher of the same sex while others, the opposite, but fully mastering the art inevitably takes a lot of time, effort and money. Compatibility is a vital ingredient in the relationship for a teacher with a gentle disposition may work well with one pupil but may be unable to draw out the latent talent in another, whereas a hard taskmaster may be exactly what a particular student needs. It is essentially a matter of authority balanced with a sympathetic understanding as young singers must always be encouraged, yet learn to accept the *'slings and arrows of outrageous misfortune'* that, when they join the profession, will inevitably come their way. Unfortunately, some young singers labour under the delusion that further vocal tuition will no longer be necessary after graduation and make a start in the profession, but a good teacher remains a mentor throughout their protégé's career, sensing and correcting faults well before the voice begins to suffer irredeemable damage.

Teachers who, at one time, had been performers in the same *fach* are a great asset as they are well aware of the vocal pitfalls and hurdles in the repertoire. Such guidance is invaluable yet it is surprising how many students fail to follow it when an audition is in the offing; inexperienced singers often take a selection of arias they love rather than those that are suitable at their current level of attainment. Having studied with a teacher for a considerable time it may be difficult to change to another without causing friction, but sometimes a change of vocal perspective is necessary and a perceptive teacher will handle the situation with integrity and grace. Some potentially promising singers never arrive at the success they had imagined because they believe in the media image of becoming a star overnight, forgetting that it takes many years to do so. Those that are impatient have a penchant for moving to different teachers if one produces a pupil who wins a competition or is contracted by a major company, so it may not be too long before teachers have to insure themselves against litigation when their pupil fails to achieve a successful career!

*C*ompetitions

Competitions range from the grass-roots Competitive Festivals long established in England (Eisteddfods in Australia), to the recent Singer of the World Competition in Cardiff, but there are many other national and international competitions, among them the Kathleen Ferrier Memorial Scholarship and the BBC's annual Young Musician of the Year. Any one of these may perhaps lead to a major career, but it is not that unusual for the winner to go no further while the runner-up or other entrants forge ahead. Competitions are something of a double-edged sword as a first prize can certainly be beneficial, but such success can result in exposure far too early with the winner having insufficient experience to withstand the pressures resulting from success. There have been instances of prizewinners accepting their very first professional engagement at an international level, who suddenly realize that they will be working with world famous stars which only shatters their self-confidence. Performers should never allow themselves to be too far in front of their current experience. Although ambition is vitally necessary to make a successful career, when excessive it can lead to disaster.

*A*uditions

Auditions are important in the early years of a career but reputation and publicity take over once a career has blossomed. It is a salutary fact that relatively few singers manage to find their way onto the first rung of the professional ladder in any one year because, from the many that audition, few are accepted. It is important for singers to present themselves with an honest (not always the case) account of their experience and to dress with circumspection, as first impressions are usually indicative. Yet, as always, there are exceptions and audition panels should avoid jumping to preconceived conclusions.

The first aria is usually of the singer's own choice; the other(s) chosen from a submitted list to the panel. This is very informative in that it often discloses whether the singer is trying to camouflage a lack of a secure top or bottom to the voice, and it always amazes audition panels how often such ploys are attempted. A teacher would point out that as an audition creates far more tension than a normal performance, it is important for the student to choose arias that are not only dramatically impressive but vocally under control as any technical weakness is immediately noticed.

Initial auditions are in front of members of the Music Staff who separate the good from the bad. More often than not their findings fall into four categories: definitely yes; 2nd or 3rd reserve; should audition again next year; and definitely no, who make up the majority of applicants. The 'definitely no' candidates include those who cannot keep in time with the accompanist or literally fizzle out before the end of the first aria; others perform an aria by Mozart as if it was by Wagner and vice versa. Some present themselves in a disheveled state as if they have slept on a park bench overnight, some overdo their appearance with too much make-up, while others attempt to impress by conversing with the panel as if they have all been bosom friends for a long time.

All is redeemed, however, when from the very first note, the panel becomes spellbound, despite having heard a superb artist singing that very same aria only the night before!

The 'definitely yes' category then have a second audition for the Musical Director and/or a representative of the Management, who may offer chorus work or a small part/understudy position with an eye to the future. Opera managements now run Young Artists Programmes for this very purpose. Working as a chorister has been previously described and young singers can learn a great deal by standing on the same stage as seasoned artists. Physical and vocal stamina, concentration, gesture, timing, working with a conductor, ensemble singing and the initiation into a vast repertoire are all valuable assets that can be absorbed while in the chorus. One of the most important lessons, however, is that the greatest artists are frequently the humblest; they do not throw their weight around and have tantrums despite the myth fostered by the media.

The Complete Rehearsal Period
Music Coaching

Coaching is undertaken by a repetiteur and occasionally by a conductor (if he or she likes to work with an artist from the very first rehearsal), depending of course on other commitments. It does happen that performers famous for specific rôles are not entirely free of musical errors which may have crept in over the years, so a refresher period with a repetiteur — especially one who imparts new insights — can be time well spent. Conversely, it has been known for stars to arrive without any preparation whatsoever and expect to master the rôle during production rehearsals. One such soprano engaged to sing the Marschallin in *Der Rosenkavalier* even had the vocal score on stage with her during the General Rehearsal. Preparing such a rôle as the

Il barbiere di Siviglia, Gioachino Rossini (Glyndebourne Touring Opera), 1994.

Conductor: Stefano Ranzani. *Director*: Aiden Lang (based on John Cox's 1981 production for the Festival). *Designer*: William Dudley.

Francisco Vas as Count Almaviva disguised as a buccaneer in order to get into Bartolo's house to abscond with Rosina.

Ermione, Gioachino Rossini, 1995.

Conductor: Andrew Davis. *Director*: Graham Vick. *Designer*: Richard Hudson.
Top row: Diana Montague as Andromache, Jorge Lopez-Yanez as Pirro, Anna Caterina Antonacci as Ermione.
Bottom Row: Gwynne Howell as Fenicio, 2 chorus members, Paul Nilon as Attalo.

This tale of passion and murder was never revived in Rossini's lifetime, but he thought very highly of the work, and was especially proud of the way the contrasting emotions of grief, love and anger were expressed musically.

The Makropulos Case, Leos Janáček, 1995

Conductor: Andrew Davis. *Director*: Nikolaus Lehnhoff. *Designer*: Tobias Hoheisal

Anja Silja as Emilia Marty the 'heroine' in one of her numerous reincarnations in this totally irrational opera.

Così fan tutte, Wolfgang Amadeus Mozart, 1996.

Conductor: Franz Weser-Most. *Director*: Trevor Nunn. *Designer*: Maria Bjørnson.
John Mark Ainsley as Ferrando, Simon Keenlyside as Guglielmo.

Cameras had not yet been invented although Mozart did relish the use of magnetism and
mesmerism in this opera.

Don Giovanni, Wolfgang
Amadeus Mozart, 2000.

Conductor: Andrew Davis.
Director: Graham Vick.
Designer: Richard Hudson.
Natale di Carolis as Don
Giovanni, Sandra Zeltzer as
Donna Elvira.

In the opera's text there is no
suggestion of any physical
intimacy between the Don
and Elvira who spends the
entire opera trying to find her
husband to save his immortal
soul while trying to come to
terms with her own desire for
him.

The Rake's Progress, Igor Stravinsky, 2000.

Conductor: Mark Elder.
Director: John Cox.
Designer: David Hockney.
1. Ryland Davies as Sellem the auctioneer.
2. *Epilogue*: Stafford Dean as Trulove, Rosemary Joshua as Anne Trulove, Richard Croft as Tom Rakewell, Susan Bickley as Baba the Turk, Gerald Finley as Nick Shadow.

Stravinsky fused his own musical style to that of Mozart and other eighteenth-century composers thereby permitting producers and designers to do likewise. Stravinsky's music is pastiche lifted to 'high art'. The Epilogue is very much in the tradition of the eighteenth-century Vaudeville. Both Ryland Davies and Stafford Dean began their careers as choristers during the author's time as Glyndebourne's Choral Director.

A Midsummer Night's Dream, Benjamin Britten, 2001.

Conductor: David Atherton. *Director*: Sir Peter Hall. *Designer*: John Bury.
Lisa Larsson as Tytania, Peter Rose as Bottom.

The scene between Tatiana and Bottom as the Ass is a highly exotic, irrational and erotic situation.

Die entführung aus dem Serail, Wolfgang Amadeus Mozart (Glyndebourne Touring Opera), 1997.
Conductor: Richard Farnes.
Director: Aiden Lang.
Designer: William Dudley.
The cast list: Belmonte – Carlo Vincenzo Allemano, Osmin – Gregory Frank, Pedrillo – Jeffrey Lloyd-Roberts, Bassa Selim – Paul Herzberg, Constanze – Ghillian Sullivan, Blonde – Mary Hegarty.

The plot – abduction from the harem – is nothing but exotic. At the time of the original production, all commentators concluded that the work demonstrated Mozart's musical and artistic maturity. It is said that it was at this production that the Emperor remarked, 'An awful lot of notes, my dear Mozart', to which Mozart replied, 'Only as many as are needed, your Majesty'.

The Bartered Bride, Bedřich Smetana, 1999.

Conductor: Jiří Kout.
Director: Nikolaus Lehnhoff.
Designer: Tobias Hoheisal.
Marisol Montalvo as Esmeralda, Wolfgang Ablinger-Sperrhacke as Vasek, Andrew Forbes-Lane as Ringmaster.

This is a 'folk' opera of spontaneous charm. The dances (a late addition) and the duets never fail to excite, and from the beginning the opera was accepted enthusiastically by audiences world-wide.

Le nozze di Figaro, Wolfgang Amadeus Mozart, 2000.

Conductor: Andrew Davies.
Director: Graham Vick.
Designer: Richard Hudson.
Andrew Shore as Bartolo.

An eighteenth-century costume for Bartolo in twentieth-century décor. The cubicle is decidedly angular whereas Mozart's music never is!

Capriccio, Richard Strauss, 1998.

Conductor: Andrew Davies. *Director*: John Cox. *Designers*: Dennis Lennon & Martin Battersby.
Felicity Lott as The Countess.

Bringing forward the production to the twentieth century was as much an anachronism as was Strauss's own penchant for an ersatz eighteenth century.

Così fan tutte, Wolfgang Amadeus Mozart, 1998.

Conductor: Andrew Davies. *Director*: Graham Vick. *Designer*: Richard Hudson.
1. Natale de Carolis as Guglielmo and Barbara Frittoli as Fiordiligi.
2. Roberto Saccà as Ferrando and Katarina Karneus as Dorabella.

As the men are minus any extra facial hair to disguise their true identity, it adds even more to the plot's original irrationality.

The Bartered Bride, Bedřich Smetana, 1999.

Conductor: Jiří Kout. *Director*: Nikolaus Lehnhoff. *Designer*: Tobias Hoheisal.

Solveig Kringelborn as Mařenka with members of the chorus.

Le Comte Ory, Gioachino Rossini, 1998.

Conductor: Yves Abel. *Director*: Jérôme Savary. *Designer*: Ezio Toffolutti.
1. Marc Laho as Comte Ory disguised as a hermit, Annick Massis as Countess Adèle.
2. Jane Shaulis as Ragonde (kneeling with handkerchief), Marc Laho as Ory, Tamsin Coombs as Alice, Ludovic Tézier as Raimbaud with members of the chorus.

With the men on a Crusade, and the women having taken a vow of chastity, coupled with mistaken identity in the dark, *Le Comte Ory* has all the ingredients of opera as sheer entertainment.

Pelléas et Mélisande, Claude Debussy, 1999.

Conductor: Andrew Davies. *Director*: Graham Vick. *Designer*: Paul Brown.

1. John Tomlinson as Golaud and Christiane Oelze as Mélisande.
2. Christiane Oelze as Mélisande.

John Tomlinson began his career as a chorister during the author's time as Glyndebourne's Choral Director. There have been many different production and design solutions to the problem of Melisande's incredibly long hair.

Pelléas et Mélisande, Claude Debussy, 1999.

Conductor: Andrew Davies. *Director*: Graham Vick. *Designer*: Paul Brown.
Richard Croft as Pelléas.

Pelléas descending into the catacombs conjures up the claustrophobic atmosphere of
Edgar Allan Poe, who had a great influence on Debussy. The composer even
contemplated an opera on 'The Fall of the House of Usher'.

Marschallin may take a considerable amount of time and nervous energy, especially when the artist is fulfilling other commitments at the same time, so the opportunity to work privately with a respected repetiteur or coach is usually welcomed.

Ensemble Rehearsals

During the ensemble rehearsals, the cast is moulded into a vocally balanced and unified musical interpretation by the conductor, or if unavailable, a repetiteur. Due to the availability of individual singers, ensemble rehearsals are sometimes minimal as it is assumed that the performers are conversant with the music, that the opera in is their repertoire, and that musical errors can be rectified during the production rehearsals. This is a fallacy because ample ensemble rehearsals are imperative, especially for Mozart's highly involved ensembles. It can be useful for producers to attend these ensemble rehearsals to familiarize themselves with the conductor's interpretation, although they should keep a low profile so as not to impinge on the conductor's domain even if they have thoroughly discussed the opera previously. At the ensemble rehearsals the conductor is busy not only with the overall interpretation but also with discovering any individual singer's foibles and special requirements, such as the time needed to breath in an unusual place. It also allows the conductor to absorb the various personalities, as ultimately a performance depends on the fusion of like minds in harmony, with the conductor being a 'chairperson' rather than a dictator.

Production Rehearsals

The number of production rehearsals varies according to the length and complexity of each opera, during which the conductor should adopt a slightly subordinate position, yet ensure that the musical ensemble is not jeopardized by 'blocking' (the ground plan of the production): namely, entrances, exits, circumnavigation of the furniture and any other practical matters. Then follows the development of the drama in greater detail based on the character of the various rôles, culminating in run-throughs of acts and the whole opera. Meanwhile, during the production period, the conductor rehearses the orchestra elsewhere so it is an opportunity for a young assistant conductor to take command and begin to work with an experienced producer.

Some conductors yearn to produce an opera as well as conduct, though it is not always advisable. The most important practical reason against this is that at the crucial time of the stage with orchestra rehearsals, the conductor has to be in the pit, and even though a production assistant may be very competent, the cast is left rudderless and unable to receive any first-hand guidance from their producer, the conductor.

Sitzprobe

The nervous tension of singing in front of orchestral colleagues at a *sitzprobe* (seated rehearsal) – even in a very familiar opera – is not always conducive to the best possible singing. It provides the singers with the first opportunity to sing through the opera without thinking about the production, but rather to absorb the instrumental timbres, and to listen out for the cues on which they will depend. The ideal venue is in the theatre itself with the singers seated on stage and the orchestra in the pit, but that is not always possible because, at the same time, the stage can be used to sort out the production's technical requirements. Instead, the *sitzprobe* might have to take place in a room reserved for production rehearsals where the acoustics often differ considerably to those in the theatre.

The ideal progression when the production rehearsals are virtually finished is for the *sitzprobe* to be scheduled after the piano dress rehearsal(s) as it is at the *sitzprobe* that the conductor is in command once more. Unfortunately the *sitzprobe* usually occurs before the piano dress rehearsal(s) to accommodate the technical rehearsals mentioned above so that the singers, having adapted to the increased sonority of the orchestra, have now to revert to the sound of the piano once more.

*P*iano Dress Rehearsal(s)

Piano dress rehearsals are still in the producer's domain chiefly because the theatre's dimensions are different to that of the rehearsal room and the sight lines, the timing of entrances and exits, and many other details, all have to be adjusted. The producer may also have to modify the singer's positions, however slightly, so that they can be in touch with the conductor at all times; incidentally, it allows the singers an opportunity to experiment with their vocal projection into the auditorium. Virtually all modern theatres have batteries of television monitors so that the conductor can be seen at all times, but even so it is frustrating for a conductor if he or she has no personal, eye-to-eye contact with the artist.

*O*rchestra Rehearsals with the Stage

This is the crucial moment for it is the first time that the conductor, the orchestra and the singers are all wedded to the production. At this point the producer accepts the uniquely operatic situation that the conductor now takes command. Problems only arise if a producer — oblivious to the fact that opera is not spoken drama — attempts major alterations, but it is usually too late to add anything new and complex. An obliging conductor will stop if necessary (though it depends on the circumstances), or if it is fortuitously useful to correct an orchestral mishap.

General (Dress) Rehearsal

The Final (General) Dress Rehearsal normally runs as per performance and some companies open it up to an invited audience. But it is not unheard of for a dress rehearsal to be halted in mid-course due to a lighting system breaking down or any other major practical problem. Even though there is an audience, it is definitely not a performance and the singers may not always 'sing out', in order to save their vocal cords for the imminent first night. An announcement is often made to that affect, but unjust criticism does tend to get bandied about; yet, when the General (Dress) Rehearsal does take wing, to electrify performers and audience alike, the opening night may turn into something of an anti-climax.

The Administration

The infrastructure of a permanent opera company is as complex as any industrial or commercial organization, the subtle difference being the end product; a commercial enterprise exists for financial and material profit whereas an opera company's avowed aim is to express the intangibility of the human spirit – be it profound, tragic, spiritual or unashamedly amusing. Unlike the straight theatre, an opera company employs a sizeable chorus, a medium to large orchestra, a music staff and an ensemble of any number of principal artists; whether large or small, permanent or seasonal, no opera company is able to function for any length of time without shrewd management and assiduous financial control. The perennial problem is to balance the budget with artistic excellence, but the former often has a habit of defeating the latter. When this occurs, tensions occur between the General Manager and the Artistic or Musical Director, so a virile Board of Directors is vitally necessary to maintain the status quo, without interfering of course in the day-to-day running of the company.

*B*oard of Directors

For a considerable period the patrons of opera were kings, princes or the aristocracy who were usually intent on outdoing their rivals, but this began to change with the rise of the bourgeoisie and the mercantile strata of society. By the eighteenth century it was the citizens of Prague rather than the aristocracy who commissioned *Don Giovanni*. *Die Zauberflöte* was likewise composed not for royalty, but to help a suburban theatre manager, Emanuel Schikaneder, who desperately needed a 'hit' to keep his theatre from financial ruin. With the industrial revolution and the commercial expansion in Europe and America during the nineteenth century, opera began to flourish as never before, aided and abetted by the wives of the wealthy tycoons who patronized the new breed of conductors (many of whom were the avid disciples of Wagner).

These autocratic Musical Directors were allowed to hire and fire singers and players at will, partly because the trade union movement had not as yet come into existence to keep them in check. At that time, Boards of Management were ostensibly unconcerned with such matters, but in more recent times this has had to change with the democratization process even though there remains something of the previous penchant for social status. The Board of Directors is now appointed from across the spectrum of commerce, politics and industry, and, in some countries, the aristocracy. Members are not always passionate opera goers but have strong connections in their particular fields (accountancy, fund raising, industrial, arts sponsorship, and government); as a result they are invaluable as the overseers of any company and its financial viability.

*C*hief Executive Officer / General *A*dministrator / General Manager / General Director / Intendant / Schauspieldirektor

Previously the holder of this office had a different title, that of Impresario, but today an Impresario implies a manager or promoter of any entertainment with little or no connection with opera. Hardly any company (if any) is now based on the principle of a triumvirate consisting of a Musical Director, a Director of Production, and a General Manager (albeit that in 1934 the Glyndebourne Festival began in exactly that way with Fritz Busch, Carl Ebert and Rudolf Bing). After the death of Fritz Busch, Glyndebourne did not continue along the same path and other companies have not followed that original and highly practical model of a triumvirate. They either engage a General Manager and a Musical Director or a GM only who then contracts the artists, including conductors. So the General Manager (CEO/GA) is the supreme authority. If a company engages a Musical Director, the General Manager usually has a place on the Board but not necessarily the Musical Director; this lays the foundation for possible strife especially if both are avid disciples of Machiavelli! Compatibility is vitally important especially if a conductor's over-inflated ego swamps that of the General Manager. But if a battle ensues, the victor is often the latter, who has closer ties with the Board, unless the former is an equally adroit politician.

To be a successful General Manager, the requirements are many, ranging from out and out tyrant to being perfectly charming yet having a strong fist within a velvet glove. A GM needs to be an adroit diplomat, for, when offering a contract to a performer from a myriad of equally good rivals, the unlucky ones have to be convinced of the many good reasons why they were not chosen! One GM even publicly admitted that underneath his hard exterior there lay a heart of stone and another maintained that it was necessary to have principles but to be prepared to ignore them when necessary!

General Managers spring from all kinds of backgrounds: some are business tycoons with perhaps little knowledge or even love of opera; others may be retired singers or have climbed the administrative ladder from that of a lowly assistant stage manager, gaining invaluable insight into the technical and artistic requirements along the way. It is an extremely stressful occupation having to overcome one crisis after another and making hard decisions regardless of personal relationships. Like any other Chief Executive, there are very few moments in any one day when a conscientious General Manager dares to be absent from the theatre.

*P*ublicity and Promotion

Promotional advertising has come a long way since the days when Wagner was prepared to lend his illustrious name to advertising Steinway Pianos: '*A Beethoven Sonata, a Bach Fantasie, can only be fully appreciated when rendered upon one of your Pianofortes.*' It has come even further since John Christie wrote the following, which he headed 'Where To Live' in the very first Glyndebourne programme in 1934. '*Why not come and live within reach of this Festival Opera House/The Opera House needs your support so that its Festivals can be extended, so that there can be more Festivals, so that there can be Concerts, so that there can be Shakespearean Festivals, so that there can be Lectures. If you come to this district you can help this scheme. You will have Downs, Sea-air, Woods and "Kultur". If you scatter yourselves over England you are too far away to support this enterprise. If you are near at hand you can enjoy superb intellectual food which you cannot get elsewhere. Make this an artistic and creative centre. You will then enjoy this marvellous country all the more. There is an excellent service of comfortable express trains to London and there are good roads for motoring. The country contains many famous schools for those who bring a family to the district.*'

Promotion for opera is as much an imperative as for any other type of entertainment, not forgetting sport, while private, industrial and commercial sponsorship is equally vital if companies are to survive. Any means is justifiable if it encourages a larger audience who previously would never have considered entering a theatre never mind an opera house. Carmen, Butterfly and Violetta are touted as call girls or prostitutes, which is a gross simplification; just as the intimacy of chamber music is promoted as 'sexy', it seems that opera has to be equally alluring! Performers have to feed the media with gossip about their private lives to titillate a potential audience, while some, like Hollywood film stars, engage publicists specifically for the purpose; it is a precarious policy because performers can easily 'arrive' before they are ready. There are many such performers whose careers have fizzled out who bear witness to the fact that however difficult it may be to open a window of opportunity, it is even more so to survive unless their talent is on a par with their ambition. To further this ambition some work hard at developing a photogenic personality to promote products ranging from perfume and watches to expensive cars – yet others achieve equal success without having to go to such lengths.

Most major opera houses now have shopping outlets for their memorabilia ranging from miniature busts of composers to perfumed toilet paper embossed with a few bars of a composer's manuscript, which is hardly the place for a work of genius! The public is bombarded with television commercials during which only the first three bars of Verdi's *La donna e mobile* are sufficient to sell tomato sauce or a helicopter gunship on the sleeve of a CD to sell *Die Götterdämmerung* as if it were a Hollywood epic. Vivaldi and Holst are used to sell a number of household articles, but Mozart reigns supreme as he is obviously very good at selling anything. As long ago as 1927, before mass media promotion had even begun, Frederick Delius wrote the following in an article, 'At the Crossroads', for the now defunct music magazine, *The Sack*, which is still relevant today: '*The average man of the present day is so accustomed to having his mind made up for him by advertisements, posters, and illuminated signs at every street corner, that he comes to believe implicitly anything he reads often enough on the hoardings . . . Anybody can do anything and call it "art" in the certain expectation of making a crowd of idiots stand and stare at him in gaping astonishment and admiration . . . !'*

Agents and Artist's Managers

Agents seek engagements for their clients whereas Artist's Managers offer a much larger area of advice in such things as suitability of the rôles offered, future artistic development, what career path to follow, and the complicated details involved in travel and accommodation. An Artist's Manager (AM) must also be a skilled negotiator with a thorough understanding of contractual legalities and have experience in all aspects of professional life. Consequently, tact and diplomacy are vital as it is difficult to explain to a client why a rival on the AM's roster has been engaged; Artist's Managers have been described as everything from marriage guidance counsellors to tax accountants. Trying to cope with a career without an agent or a manager, a performer can easily find himself enmeshed in contractual difficulties unless they are adept at reading the small print. Instances have been known of inexperienced singers signing up with unscrupulous agents who then charge them exorbitant commission but fail to find the right opportunities for them at that stage of their careers. Although the difference between an Agent and an Artist's Manager is quite marked, some inexperienced artists confuse the two.

An Artist's Manager's relationship with the administration varies on whether the company employs an Artistic Director/Music Director as well as a General Manager or only a GM, though contracts are usually negotiated with an Artistic Administrator. Artistic Directors and AMs like to meet on a fairly regular basis to discuss overall casting, the development of individual artists and how they might fit into the company's future plans. Such meetings are useful also to discuss new, potential artists who may have only recently joined the AM's roster. When trust has been well and truly established, confidential discussions can then take place about concerns the company may have regarding an artist so that the AM can advise their protégé accordingly. Commission rates vary from country to country but as a yardstick the Australian standard rate for each performance during a season of opera is 10 percent and occasionally less if a longer contract has been negotiated; for a one-off concert or recital, it is usually around 15 percent.

Government and/or State Funding

Tradition and economics have both played an important part in operatic funding. In Germany, just one major company receives considerably more state funding than the whole of the performing arts in most if not all other European countries. It stems from the fact that the Germans have a pride in their operatic heritage whether the mass of the population is interested or not. Going to the opera is a tradition that has existed for over two hundreds years. When the Second World War ended, many German opera houses were rebuilt before other 'worthy' institutions because opera was and still is considered a public facility along with gas, electricity, health and education.

England never had a similar tradition until the Arts Council was specifically formed to rectify the deficiency immediately after the Second World War, and even then the funding was very small compared to that in Germany. Glyndebourne was very much the exception in that it came into existence thanks to the vision and financial resources of one man, John Christie, who scorned the very idea of state subsidy. But by 1939 his private funding was being somewhat stretched beyond its limits. Rudolf Bing, Glyndebourne's General Manager, who was classed as an alien at the time, was permitted to work in a London department store where he discovered that the store was beginning to develop sponsorship of the arts. The logical outcome was that when the Glyndebourne Festival recommenced after the war, commercial and industrial sponsorship – coupled with a programme book with extensive advertising – was gradually instituted. Glyndebourne has survived ever since with only the occasional and minimal financial difficulty, while some state-supported companies have suffered badly during lean years. In 1968, when the Touring Company was established, the Arts Council ignored John Christie's original scorn and supported the young company so that the opera-going public around the country could enjoy Glyndebourne's highly acclaimed productions.

If opera is a luxury then so must be all other forms of art and entertainment, including sport, which receives substantial financial sponsorship. The German example shows that opera really is not a luxury but a necessity in any 'civilized' community for, after all, Man cannot live by bread alone!

The Audience

When the editor of a musical journal asked Verdi if he, like Wagner, had any specific theories about opera, his reply was typically to the point: *'Yes, the theatre should be full.'*

Applause

It is ironic that when a performance finishes, the sound in the auditorium is superseded by the noise of clapping, even if it seems to be heaven-sent music to the performer. Applause is vitally important as ego nourishment, a stimulus and a prognostication of a likely future (and fees), the yardstick being that one is only as good as one's last performance. In 1773, the castrato Farinelli was highly incensed because his London audience could not contain itself and applauded for all of five minutes, yet he had only sung one note! Early in the nineteenth century, some members of the Milanese audience equipped themselves with sticks and banged them on the wooden seats to express their delight, and people in the gallery threw down leaflets inscribed with sonnets in praise of the performers. In 1868 in Ireland, after a soprano finished her aria in Weber's *Oberon*, the applause went on for a quarter of an hour and only died down after she promised to sing *The Last Rose of Summer*. A piano was brought on stage to accompany her as there were no orchestral parts in the theatre. Verdi was so taken aback by the tremendous applause at a première that he could only exclaim *'Heavens! What's the matter with it?'* Even today it is not that unusual for an aria to be ruined by vociferous applause well before the orchestra has finished playing the postlude, the classic examples being the arias in *Don Giovanni* for Zerlina and Don Ottavio.

Mozart was well aware of the need to encourage the audience. In a letter to his father dated 1781 he wrote, *'A great deal of noise is always appropriate at the end of an act. The more noise the better, and the shorter the better, so that the audience has no time to cool down with their applause.'* Berlioz, in his *Les Soirées de l'orchestre* (Seventh Evening), included a satirical episode on clapping techniques and hand positions of his day. One type was the different intensity needed by a prima donna's husband to that of her lover; the lover should not to be too boisterous in case the husband suspected an affair, but if a husband clapped too loudly it might influence the management's deliberations concerning his wife's fee!

The claque system still exists to a certain extent and as recently as 1931 the French press printed the conditions by which an Italian tenor would agree to sing; he demanded a claque to be engaged and favourable reviews to be written. Some sections of audiences indulge in shouts of 'Bravo' and 'Brava' (feminine), depending on the perspicacity of the cognoscenti; others stamp their feet and some even let out high pitched whistles. Booing is a German tradition and seems to erupt as a matter of course regardless of whether the performance is good or bad. Kurt Weill's *Mahagonny* was greeted with rotten eggs while in Italy, crockery, fruit and vegetables were all used at one time or another. In the eighteenth century, oranges were the favourite missiles; the composer Pergolesi was once bespattered with them. Wagner banned clapping in Bayreuth as he considered it irreverent in his profoundly 'religious' atmosphere yet at Rossini's funeral, attended by 6,000 mourners, a chorus sang the Prayer from his *Mose in Egitto* and encored it despite the solemn occasion. At one time singers were expected to provide encores as a matter of course but they have virtually disappeared today so as not to interrupt the dramatic continuity; encore literally means 'repeat' or 'again'.

Surtitles

When surtitles were introduced during the latter half of the twentieth century they were accepted as a mixed blessing – welcomed by some but castigated by others. For a member of an audience with little or no knowledge of the original language, surtitles convey the meaning of the text concurrently with the music, but concentration on the stage is destroyed by the continual search for the text above the proscenium arch. One famous Diva even commented that her audiences were being short-changed because at least half of her illustrious performance was being lost!

Surtitles are now accepted as a matter of course even when the opera is sung in English, whether in translation or in the original language. In the past, English singers only needed a reproach for slovenly diction and they corrected it, but, knowing full well that the audience can see the surtitles, they now unconsciously excuse their bad enunciation. That is not to deny that some composers sustain a word over a long phrase for viable musical reasons and any vocal ensemble from two, to eight or more parts increases the difficulty of clarity, and therefore comprehension.

The Music Critic

Audience response is vitally necessary for both the performers and the overall production, but its intensity may fluctuate during the course of an evening. It subtly affects performers one way or another, inspiring them to greater heights or the opposite, as performing is a subjective art. A performance may feel splendid to those on stage yet fail to ignite the audience or it may be damned by the critics but adored by the audience; alternatively the critics may praise a work to the skies yet the audience might stay away in droves. There seems to be no criterion and the old saying *'I like what I know and know what I like'* is actually quite valid despite being ridiculed in some quarters.

Whereas music critics review concerts and drama critics the theatre, more often than not drama critics do not review opera even though its visual realization should be considered in relation to its music. A music critic may not be dramatically attuned and a tone-deaf drama critic should not review opera, but a good music critic should understand the totality of music and drama that is opera – how it differs from the straight theatre and the different performing skills required, both on stage and in the orchestra pit.

Music critics themselves are sometimes criticized for having little knowledge of their subject but, as mentioned in connection with producers, critics may be musical but not necessarily skilled in musicianship. Critical qualities were admirably explained by Fred Blanks on his retirement from the *Sydney Morning Herald* in 1996. *'Criticism of the arts is not an international conspiracy against creativity, but when practiced with integrity it is a constructive promotion of understanding between the creator of art and its beholder. A music critic must love music. A critic asks himself whom he is addressing.*

He is not an agent for composers, performers or promoters, though they all find him useful when he plays their tune. He is primarily responsible to his medium and readers. Unfortunately, the media — no exceptions — are replacing such critical assessment with the kind of pre-digested commercial puffery which advertisers cherish. The reasons are, of course, financial . . . Critics strike a fine balance between objectivity and subjectivity.'

Readers of criticism do not always realize that a review, however objective, is fundamentally one person's opinion of that particular performance. It is inevitably coloured by the critic's subjectivity on that occasion as with any other member of the audience. Agents and General Managers use reviews for their own purposes, quoting a good one to promote artists and ignoring a bad one when expediency demands. Performers, on the other hand, are flattered by the smallest compliment and furious at the opposite, but logically, if they are prepared to accept the former as reasonable, then the latter is equally valid! What may appear on first reading to be bad or scurrilous, when read again (after a lapse of time), has a chameleon-like habit of becoming innocuous and even complimentary. A constructive handling of a bad review is to accept that perhaps there is a grain of truth lying hidden in it and to use it as a springboard for further development. Some performers are so strong minded that they never read reviews, good or bad (or at least profess not to), but the temptation is overpowering.

There is an unwritten law in the profession never to publicly reply to a critic for the obvious reason that the critic always has the last word in print which may result in a disastrous later career for the artist. One such recipient dared to put pen to paper and wrote, *'I am sitting in the smallest room in the house with your review in front of me. Soon it will be behind me!'*

Interlude: Operatic Mishaps and Other Cautionary Tales

The annals of opera are littered with stories and legends some of which are true and some, outrageously fictional. But the author can vouch for the following.

During the 1967 Glyndebourne tour of Scandinavia, *Don Giovanni* was performed in the Drottningholm Court Theatre. Using the theatre's baroque unique sets, the Commendatore's statue rose out of the stage on a little plinth for the Cemetery Scene in Act 2. Unfortunately the plinth lurched as it came up and finally stuck at an angle of 45 degrees so that the 'statue' had to spend the entire scene on an incline. This did not deter Leporello, who, being something of a daredevil, got down on his hands and knees and held the candle (a naked flame) to read the inscription under the Commendatore's nose. The statue, being only human, sweated profusely throughout the scene but never moved a muscle.

‖: :‖

In a Southampton cinema on another tour, the exquisite 'Clare de Lune' that concludes Act I of Massenet's *Werther* was spiced up a little by the ice cream/cigarette lady who appeared in a doorway under the stage and wended her way through the woodwind and brass to reach the front of the stalls. She was then at the ready with her torch illuminating her presence for the imminent interval. It was her regular job be it for a film or an opera, and she was certainly not going to be found wanting!

‖: :‖

Whenever the ravishing horn solo that launches the Overture to *Ariadne auf Naxos* begins, it is touch and go whether the player will circumnavigate the difficult solo without blemish. At one performance (again on tour) as he put the horn to his lips, the emergency exit doors were flung open by a raving drunk outside who shouted the wildest obscenities. Not one solitary note of the horn solo materialized on that occasion.

‖: :‖

Cimarosa's *Il matrimonio segreto* was being staged in a university auditorium normally used as a lecture theatre with steps from the floor level to the stage. Suddenly, in the middle of the dress rehearsal, firemen came down the aisles in their burnished helmets with hatchets and hoses, then moved through the orchestra, up the steps on to the stage where the cast (unperturbed) was singing, and out through a door in the set; the scene was straight out of a Marx Brothers' film. On enquiry after the rehearsal it transpired that the arc lights that had been brought in especially for the performance had activated the alarm in the local fire station. The conductor was assured that it would not happen again but on the first night, it did!

‖: :‖

For the very first Bayreuth Festival in 1876 a canvas dragon was ordered for Faffner from a factory in Birmingham, England, but it never arrived. In 1928, a moth eaten, rotting piece of sacking was discovered in a warehouse in Beirut, Lebanon; it was the missing Faffner.

‖: :‖

A 'perpetual' understudy in a provincial German opera house was finally allowed to prove her worth as Leonore in *Fidelio*. To make the greatest possible impression, she spat out the first word of the recitative *'Abscheulicher!'* (Horrible, disgusting) with such tremendous force that her dentures shot out and she spent the whole aria groping around the stage for them. It was her first and last engagement as a principal.

‖: :‖

Another understudy situation occurred in *Carmen*. The principal Escamilio fell ill and, as the understudy wanted to make an impression with something spectacular, he jumped onto a table in

Lillas Pastia's tavern and with great aplomb danced as he sang the Toreador's Aria. Having heard of the understudy's spectacular tour de force, the principal Escamilio quickly returned to health and, to reclaim his glory, attempted the same Hollywood film-like gesture but crashed through the flimsy table and had to sing encased in it. The understudy left town before the opera finished that night to avoid Escamilio's wrath and fury.

‖: :‖

In a rather ramshackle opera company, Gounod's *Faust* was scheduled but the sets could only be erected on the afternoon of the first night. An alert carpenter noticed that the window of Margeurite's house kept opening and shutting so he put a latch inside the window frame to hold it still. During the performance, Marguerite was unable to open the window to sing the duet with Faust. Realizing the problem, the quick-thinking tenor surreptitiously put his hand up under the flimsy canvas to turn the latch but his fingers managed to find their way inside Margeurite's dress where they twiddled around searching for the recalcitrant latch. On that occasion, the duet was performed with the soprano in something of a predicament.

‖: :‖

A petulant Diva always refused to re-rehearse the role for which she was world famous. At one opera house, despite the Stage Manager's difficult task of trying to inform her about their particular set, she would not listen so was totally unprepared for a towering glass staircase that had been built especially for her spectacular entrance. The Diva appeared at the very top in full regal splendour and then proceeded to slide all the way down, bumping and bruising her extremities as she went!

Opera Companies

Festival Opera

Opera Festivals are now a well established feature in Europe and America at such locations as Salzburg, Glyndebourne, Wexford, Santa Fe, Bregenz and Aix en Provence, to name only a few of the most celebrated. The principals, chorus and orchestra all come together for an intensive rehearsal period to perform a repertoire unique to that company or area or may concentrate on one composer. Since its inception in 1934, Glyndebourne has always had a reputation for Mozart, despite the fact that it has covered a wide spectrum from Monteverdi, Gluck, Rossini, Verdi and Tchaikovsky to Debussy, Prokofiev, Britten, Stravinsky and, surprisingly, Gershwin. Its founder, John Christie, had originally wanted to perform Wagner and expected the male members of the audience to wear lederhosen and the females, dirndls. Perhaps due to its initial artistic directors, Carl Ebert and Fritz Busch, John Christie's *exotic and irrational* request was conveniently ignored. During the early years of the Wexford Festival the Italian *bel canto* repertoire was extensively explored, but the festival later branched out into the lesser-known repertoire of other periods. Pesaro, Rossini's birthplace, naturally concentrates on his vast output including not only the comic operas for which he is most famous but his serious operas as well. Seattle and Adelaide specialize in Wagner festivals.

Repertory and Stagione Companies

The four most famous opera houses in the world are La Scala, Milan; the Metropolitan, New York; the Vienna Staatsoper; and the Royal Opera House, Covent Garden. Berlin, however, has three opera houses, all having very strong international reputations and each specializing in a particular style: Die Deutsche Opera for contemporary works; Die Komische Opera – despite its name – performs serious and radical operas; and Die Staatsoper, more traditional repertoire. Germany also has many companies with variable standards ranging from Hamburg, Stuttgart, Frankfurt and Munich at the very top to those of quite small provincial towns. France can boast a number of excellent companies and the capital has two major houses, the Paris Opera (described by Debussy as looking like a railway station on the outside and a Turkish bath on the inside) and the Opera Bastille, which has been regularly embroiled in controversy. In America, the most famous companies apart from the Metropolitan at the Lincoln Center are the New York City Opera and the San Francisco Opera. Most state capitals mount opera seasons based on the popular operas. In Russia the major company is the Bolshoi, in Buenos Aires the Teatro Colon, in Brussels the Monnaie, and in London the English National Opera. Scotland has Scottish Opera and Wales, The Welsh National Opera, both with very high standards.

There are many other companies all over Europe and America providing excellent seasons without necessarily reaching the same level as those mentioned above. The Canadian Opera is based in Toronto and there are companies in Ottawa, Vancouver, Winnipeg Calgary and French seasons in Montreal and Quebec. Australia's operatic 'flagship' is Opera Australia (previously The Australian Opera) based in Sydney, which is recognized as the national company yet the only other city in which it performs is Melbourne. Brisbane, Adelaide and Perth all have seasons based on the stagione system.

Seasonal and Semi-permanent Companies

Stagione (seasonal) companies function with a resident roster of singers and invited guest artists. They perform for most of the year with a repertoire of usually no more than five operas in rotation and have to be geared to the box-office as well as receiving government subsidy. The less popular operas are included from time to time so as not to artistically stagnate, but a careful balance between artistic enterprise and budgetary considerations has to be maintained at all times.

Most of these companies employ the city's symphony orchestra and an enthusiastic amateur chorus which, incidentally, provides excellent apprenticeship opportunities for aspiring performers. Agents and Administrators are always on the look out for new talent so these companies are the grass roots from which they select the next generation of singers for their own Young Artists programmes.

Production Sharing

As a result of today's financial climate, it is now eminently logical for companies to share their productions, even between continents, as for instance Britten's *Billy Budd* for the Welsh National Opera and Opera Australia in Sydney and Melbourne. The original producer usually directs the opera for both companies with the same basic sets. The production is modified if necessary to suit the different conditions but the conductor and cast are almost certain to be the resident performers.

Touring

Touring companies, like the Carl Rosa and others, used to employ many artists but financial constraints have caused such companies to disappear. Only a few companies dare undertake international tours and then principally as cultural ambassadors for their respective countries. In its earliest years, Glyndebourne Touring Opera (GTO) always performed opera productions that had been first presented at the Festival, but more recently the GTO has branched out with its own original productions.

Opera Australia used to tour to all the state capitals but as air travel, living and accommodation allowances on top of normal salaries are astronomical, the company now only travels to Melbourne. A European equivalent would be for Covent Garden to visit Berlin, Moscow and even distant Tokyo on a regular basis! The grass roots of the operatic world include very small companies, usually just with piano accompaniment. Nevertheless, such companies provide valuable experience for graduating students to bridge the gap between the termination of their studies and the unknown and untried professional world.

Although not considered touring, open-air performances have now become a fact of operatic life with *Tosca* performed in its original location – where the drama never took place – and *Turandot* performed in the Forbidden City in Beijing. Other open-air operas range from the gargantuan performances in Verona to Australia's *al fresco* 'Opera in the Outback' consisting of the most popular arias and songs from opera and musicals performed for an audience who dress up for the occasion and have picnics as if they were at Glyndebourne minus its green meadows and lush lakes. This is now the age in which opera is exploited for innumerable commercial reasons with whatever gimmick an adroit entrepreneur can think up: The Three Tenors, The Three Chinese Tenors, etc. Australia has its own non-sexist version, the Three Divas!

'Peoples' Opera

An unfortunate victim of the increased costs has been the demise of 'peoples' opera that held ticket prices to within reasonable limits for the less affluent members of society. Sadlers Wells Opera thrived for many years on a varied repertoire. Its successor, The English National Opera, having moved to the larger Coliseum in the West End of London, was compelled to charge higher prices. The 'blue-collar' workers no longer felt comfortable and they virtually vanished to make way for a middle-class intelligentsia. Inevitably, this led to much greater financial problems and the never-ending search for a larger subsidy from the government.

Television Opera

The past thirty or forty years has seen great progress in the quality of opera on television both as outside broadcasts from opera houses and studio productions. The major problem during the early days of television was the location of the orchestra because the recording studios were set up for cameras with extended cables so positioning an orchestra in this set-up was well nigh impossible. The BBC attempted to solve the problem by having the orchestra in another studio which meant that the orchestral sound had to be relayed into the studio at the lowest possible level or it spilt over into the microphones. The singers had to depend entirely on an assistant conductor who followed the principal conductor on a monitor while moving around the studio following the cameras without being caught on screen. Meanwhile, the principal conductor and the orchestra had little, if any, contact with the singers. If a visual mistake occurred there would be a retake – but never when the music came adrift.

Later studio recordings experimented with the sound being

pre-recorded to which the singers mimed with an occasional lack of synchronization or an obvious lack of larynx involvement. Benjamin Britten resisted many invitations to compose an opera especially for television until the BBC agreed to the orchestra being with the singers in the same studio. *Owen Wingrave* was the result. Live relays from opera houses have also come along way since the early days, with Glyndebourne leading the way. But for the first attempts from Sussex, the cameramen had to wear black bow ties and dinner jackets like any other member of the audience.

Opera on Video

Video and DVD recordings have now been developed to such an extent that first-class performances can be enjoyed in the comfort of one's own home at far less cost than going to the theatre and all that entails. *Le nozze di Figaro* and *The Queen of Spades* from the Metropolitan Opera are just two of the many superb opera video recordings now readily available. As a direct result of this technology, many more people can now experience opera than have ever set foot in opera houses during the past three hundred years. It has also led to great progress being made in presentation by compelling operatic casting to be more conscious of physical appearance, as the small screen does not tolerate facial contortions. The camera is very revealing so opera on video is a somewhat different concept to opera in the theatre where distance (sometimes) lent enchantment. The ramifications of DVD and video will be further examined at the end of the following section.

Past, Present and Future?

The precursors of what became known as opera can be traced back to the fifteenth and sixteenth centuries and were essentially based on religious or moral subjects. The *Moralities* personified virtue and vice, and the *Miracle Plays* depicted the lives of the saints; in Italy they were called *Sacre Rappresentazioni*. Yet, despite the power of the omnipresent Roman Catholic Church – far from being the personification of evil – in parts of Europe Satan was portrayed as a downright comic character.

In Elizabethan England the aristocracy preferred more secular entertainments so the *Moralities* and *Miracle Plays* were replaced by the *Masque* and the *Pastoral*, which had far greater relevance to their decidedly secular world. The *Masque* involved speech, poetry, vocal and instrumental music, pageantry, spectacle and dance, while the *Pastoral* extolled the simple, unsophisticated life of the countryside and occasional mythological subjects. In his Diary of 1645, John Evelyn described such entertainments as '*One of the most magnificent and expensive diversions the wit of man can invent*'. Eleven years later the first English opera was performed – *The Siege of Rhodes* (its music is lost) – and in 1660, after the departure of Oliver Cromwell and the Restoration of the Monarchy, theatrical entertainments were again permitted.

Meanwhile the Palace of Versailles was built by Louis XIV to become the most celebrated in Europe followed by the Académie Royale de Musique. Paris was now the focus of European theatre and music. Louis XIV however invited a foreigner, the Italian Giovanni Battista Lulli (1632–87), to be his court musician and compose operas specifically to glorify his reign, so Lulli adopted French citizenship and changed his name to Jean-Baptise Lully. His orders were that every opera must begin with the gods descending from heaven to extol the virtues of the greatest king who ever lived. As Lully the French Prima Donnas neglected the drama in favour of vocal display, they had to be more disciplined. Lully banned all vocal ornamentation so as not to distract the audience from the most important and dramatic subject of all, *Le Roi de Soleil*. After Lully's death, vocal excess gradually re-emerged and it took approximately a hundred years before Gluck was able to reinstate Lully's reforms. The drama became paramount once again, but operatic history has been repeating this cycle ever since.

The seventeenth century was one of scientific advancement and commercial expansion, with the establishment of the English East India and Hudson Bay companies; the French exploration of Canada; Germany opening its first coffee-houses; and London erecting street lamps burning oil. In 1685, Isaac Newton discovered gravity and the French Huguenots, fearing persecution, sought asylum in England, Holland and Germany, and took their arts with them. Such was the social atmosphere of the second half of the century and in 1689, Purcell's *Dido & Aeneas* was performed for the first time. Composed for a girls' school, it included both dancers and singers like the earlier *Masques*. As well as composing a work of intense beauty, Purcell included a number of Passacaglia in which the bass line is continuously repeated, while above the vocal phrases overlap in the form of variations. Later operatic composers virtually abandoned the passacaglia until Benjamin Britten – a great admirer of Purcell – revived the form for *Peter Grimes*, *The Turn of the Screw* and his final masterpiece, *Death in Venice*.

Handel (1685–1759), a German by birth, became an English citizen and composed in the Italian style. As his vocal music became increasingly florid, excess began to re-emerge with the castrati (in the female roles) reveling in their own virtuosity at the expense of the drama. One female soprano actually cross-dressed in order to impersonate a castrato and achieved fame as a *castrato-prima donna!*

The English 'lower classes' – today's blue-collar workers – created their own theatrical entertainment, Ballad Operas, to satirize their 'betters'. Ballad Operas used contemporary popular street airs and folk tunes with new, ribald texts interspersed with dialogue. They always concluded with a Vaudeville sung by each character in turn and directed at the audience. In 1728, John Gay presented his *The Beggar's*

Opera which was a great success, but only that particular opera and its sequel *Polly* have survived to the present day. The former has inspired many such entertainments, the most popular being Kurt Weills's *Dreigroschenoper*. The Vaudeville was later used by Mozart and his librettist, Gottlieb Stephanie, for *Die Entführung aus dem Serail* but without the satirical nature of the previous Ballad Operas. Mozart and Lorenzo da Ponte, Stephanie's successor, developed it even further in *Le nozze di Figaro, Don Giovanni* and *Così fan tutte* without calling it Vaudeville. It is interesting to note that they discarded the designation of Vaudeville although Beaumarchais' original play — on which *Le nozze di Figaro* was based — did actually conclude with one.

The *Ballad Opera* had its Italian counterpart in *Commedia dell'Arte* (Comedy of Art) which exploited the streetwise characters of Harlequin, Colombine, Zanni, Pantelone, Brighella and Truffaldino, and a whole host of others. The performances were very stylized ranging from the smart man about town and the virtuous young maiden, to the crooked lawyer, the quack doctor and other ribald and earthy characters. They were the prototypes of the eighteenth century's *opera buffa* — Leporello, Dr. Bartolo, Basilio, Don Pasquale and Malatesta (Italian for bad head). *Commedia dell'Arte* performers were often banished from respectable society and the Catholic Church went so far as to excommunicate some of them for such lewd entertainments with which they toured Italy hoping to earn a meagre living.

In Germany, the counterpart of the English *Ballad Opera* was the *Singspiel* but the educated mercantile class (bourgeoisie) preferred their opera to be entirely sung and retained the recitative and aria form, perhaps to emulate the more aristocratic operatic entertainments. Being the Age of Enlightenment, Reason began to infiltrate opera and music in general, which led to the theatre becoming a near equal to the church in popularity. Consequently, the contrapuntal nature of church music — based on a single subject (the fugue) — underwent metamorphosis to become more harmonically orientated with the interplay of two (or more) contrasting subjects. Out of this new conception of music grew the keyboard sonata and the symphony. In 1759, Haydn – familiarly known as 'the father of the symphony' – composed his first, and would go on to compose over a hundred. With harmony (vertical) as opposed to counterpoint (horizontal) as the basis, melody and accompaniment began to dominate vocal music so that opera flourished even more than before.

The next decade saw the first stirrings of the North American colonists with the Boston Tea Party, until independence was finally won from England albeit that the vast majority of Europeans were uninterested in the struggle. They were more concerned with the opening up of worldwide exploration and the building of trading empires. Little did they realize that the new United States of America would profoundly effect the whole course of music in the twentieth century. Meanwhile the European intelligentsia preferred their opera to be sung in Italian rather than in their own language. It was at this time that Dr. Johnson published his *Lives of the Poets* in which he observed that opera was *'an exotic and irrational entertainment which has always been combated, and always has prevailed'*.

Although opera in France was sung in French, opera was performed in Italian in the German-speaking countries and other parts of Europe. In 1782, the Austrian Emperor decreed that a National Theatre was to be established in which opera had to be sung in German. The twenty-six-year-old Mozart obliged with *Die Entführung aus dem Serail* but despite the Emperor's decree, opera in German only lasted a year because his Viennese subjects strongly objected. *Die Entführung aus dem Serail* was then translated into Italian as *Il Seraglio* and only recently did it revert to German in most, but not all, opera companies. Although it was composed as a *singspiel*, and apart from its benign overlord, Bassa Selim, the plot was chiefly concerned with what is known in England as the 'middle class'. It certainly included the *exotic* characters of Blonde and Osmin, an exceedingly pert English lady's maid and the keeper of the harem. The opera also poked fun at the Ottoman conquerors of Eastern Europe and even as recently as 1970, audiences in that part of Europe still booed Osmin whenever he appeared on stage.

With *Le nozze di Figaro* (1786) Mozart and his new librettist, Lorenzo da Ponte, took social relevance a stage further in their portrayal of the struggle between a Count and his valet for everyone in the audience to observe. The valet's name, Figaro, was originally Figuaro in Spanish, which actually meant one who mocked his so-called 'betters'. Beaumarchais had exploited this double entendre in *Le Marriage de Figaro*, which had considerable influence on the political climate of the time and was soon – three years after Mozart's opera – to erupt into the French Revolution. Mozart and his librettist expunged most of the political implications in *Le Marriage de Figaro* and, though banned in Vienna, *Le nozze di Figaro* was first performed only two years after the play had been presented in Paris. From the very opening scene, the opera exudes a more natural feeling than had ever been portrayed before in opera. One can imagine Mozart himself pacing up and down, searching for the timing and the right musical shape as Figaro measures the ante-chamber – a room provided by the Count allowing him access to Susanna at any time.

Don Giovanni (1787) explored another social taboo – the sexual libertine. Don Juan and his eventual downfall had been used before by many playwrights, librettists and composers, but Mozart and da Ponte fused its serious and supernatural connotations with sensuality and earthy humour to produce a *dramma giocosa* (humorous drama). After the Don's descent into hell and damnation, Mozart had originally intended the remaining characters to rush on stage to conclude the opera but he had second thoughts; he added a Vaudeville (shorn of its title), its moral directed pointedly at the audience as if to say, 'there but for the grace of God go you'! During the nineteenth century this final scene was abandoned and a coffin containing the dead body of Donna Anna was brought on stage while her mourners sang the *Dies Irae* from the Requiem, which in fact, Mozart had not yet composed!

    Così fan tutte (1790) was similarly concerned with sexuality but the conflict implied by its title and the subtitle *Le scuola degli ammanti* (The School for Lovers) was worlds away from *Don Giovanni*. It is said to have been inspired by Mozart's own romantic liaisons with the daughters of Fridolin Weber, Aloysia and his eventual wife, Constanze. Gone were references to the monarchy or the aristocracy, and instead the comings and goings of the well-to-do, middle strata of society; as in any household of the time, the characters sing a canon during the wedding festivities, although in this instance one of them sulks about the change in their romantic relationships. It is a further example of 'necessity being the mother of artistic invention' for the vocal range of the canon is too high for a baritone. Mozart and Da Ponte treated this fundamentally serious subject of fidelity in such a lighthearted way that Beethoven and many others were scandalized by its immorality and thought it to be a sheer waste of Mozart's genius. Nineteenth-century France was equally scandalized and in 1863 Barbier and Carré, Gounod's librettists for *Faust*, liberally adapted Mozart's music so as to fit their version of Shakespeare's *Love's Labour's Lost*. Unfortunately for operatic posterity, Da Ponte left Vienna immediately after the première because Adriana Ferrarese del Bene, the opera's Fiordiligi (and his mistress), was sacked for unprofessional conduct. As a result, one of the most successful collaborations in all of opera came to an abrupt end for reasons which had nothing to do with music.

    Mozart took a metaphorical step backwards to the earlier *opera seria* style with *La clemenza di Tito*, which had to be composed in great haste – on the journey from Vienna to Prague – assisted by his pupil Franz Xaver Süssmayr for the coronation of the Emperor Leopold as the new King of Bohemia. Concurrently with *La clemenza di Tito*, Mozart had begun *Die Zauberflöte* which was a return to another former style, the *singspiel*. But he had grave doubts about being able to compose a *Zauberopera* (magic opera), then all the rage in Vienna. Schikaneder managed to persuade him and *Die Zauberflöte* proved to be an instant success with the 'groundlings', fellow Freemasons and the public at large. The source of Mozart's abiding popularity as an operatic composer – at least from the twentieth century on – has been due to his uncanny ability to musically portray fully rounded, real human beings. Cherubino, Almaviva, Susanna, Figaro, Dorabella, Guglielmo, Papageno, Tamino, Sarastro and even the Queen of the Night can all be seen walking the streets of New York, Paris, Berlin, yet a contemporary critic wrote that Mozart was a noisy, dissonant composer with no talent in writing for the voice!

'No man is an island'. So Mozart's music was subconsciously influenced by the social upheavals in Europe. His earlier operas had been constructed around the customary formula of aria/recitative/aria, but from *Idomeneo* onwards he began to experiment with what later became *durchkomponiert* (through composition). He abandoned the barriers between some of the orchestral cadences and the following *secco recitative* so scenes began to flow between the orchestra and the continuo and back again. From *Die Entführung* on, his Finales were *durchkomponiert* and extended way beyond other composer's attempts at Finales to become a model of writing for the German Romantic composers of the next century. They were also to dispense with the harpsichord-accompanied recitatives, but in Italy this new concept took longer to achieve acceptance. Both Rossini and Donizetti continued to compose *secco* (dry) recitatives before Verdi finally jettisoned the harpsichord accompaniment, though he retained the recitative with orchestral accompaniment.

The closing decade of the eighteenth century saw the rise of Napoleon who was to crown himself Emperor after the turmoil of both the French Revolution and the Reign of Terror. Beethoven's *Fidelio* – originally under the name of *Leonore* – was premièred within a few years and its political connotations have remained highly relevant ever since. Beethoven was always deeply moved by his fellow man's struggle for freedom, and in *Fidelio* this was clearly enunciated with the many reiterations of the word *Freiheit* (freedom). The opera's libretto was based on a real incident that took place during the Reign of Terror, but to avoid incrimination it was transplanted to an *exotic* country, Spain. As well as its political and social implications *Fidelio* might also be considered autobiographical, in that like Florestan, Beethoven was incarcerated, his imprisonment being the solitary confinement of deafness without any hope of *freiheit*.

After Napoleon's second exile in 1815, a period of comparative social stability reigned. Opera seasons were the entertainment highlights of the social year with Rossini achieving an unheard of success matched only by today's idols of sport and pop music. Opera houses became the places in which to be seen in a perennial quest to enhance one's social status. In Paris, the Jockey Club had their lavish boxes so that they could comfortably relish their selection of favourite paramours from the opera ballet as a prelude to a later rendezvous, but even that decidedly unmusical pastime had an affect on the composition of opera. Composers were compelled to insert ballets into their operas, placed at the start of Act 2, to allow the Jockey Club to look over prospective mistresses and latecomers to arrive after their wining and dining during the Interval. The opera ballet was without any dramatic significance so Wagner deliberately placed his Venusberg music in *Tannhäuser* at the beginning of the opera for its Paris première. This so annoyed the Jockey Club, who had little time to study their 'fillies' form, that the opera was hissed off the stage. Only after the club was disbanded did Wagner dare to replace his ballet music with the Venusburg music as now performed, while the original score sounds as if Donizetti had written it; maybe that was Wagner's intention! Verdi's *Macbeth* and some of his other early operas also had to be interrupted for a ballet, which are now usually cut, but the ballet in his later *Aida* is very much a part of the dramatic spectacle.

The same era saw the emergence of the *claque* in France, their equivalent of the Italian '*Gente pagata per applaudire*', as described previously. Amusing as the claque system may seem in these more enlightened times, they were the precursors of today's promotional departments who bombard the public long before the singer has sung a note or, on occasion, even set foot in the city! The patrons of La Scala in Milan often took their chefs to the opera to provide them with delicious refreshments during the '*aria del sorbetto*', while Protestant England was firmly convinced that any opera singer – especially from Italy – was an immoral vagabond or worse, a Papist! In central Europe, the theatre was such a hotbed of revolutionary ideas that the Austrian Emperor ordered that bows and arrows had to be used in place of muskets in *Der Freischütz* to protect him from possible assassination. In 1828, Auber's *La muette de Portici* – the first Grand Opera – had its première in Brussels, and as a result, revolution broke out within two years. Its hero, Masaniello, had inspired the Belgians' struggle for freedom from foreign domination. Curiously, and somewhat *irrationally*, Auber himself never attended a performance of his very many operas!

The next twenty years saw further political unrest and in 1848 socialist revolutions began to erupt in a number of European countries – the same year as *The Communist Manifesto* by Marx and Engels was published. The young Richard Wagner, who had been an ardent supporter of socialist ideals, abandoned his principles and fled Germany in the hope of finding a wealthy patron and the artistic success for which he desperately yearned. Besides being his own librettist, Wagner was an inspiring conductor and an ardent (sometimes virulent) pamphleteer on a vast array of subjects including German politics. His writings were instrumental in rousing German patriotic sentiment and they finally bore fruit in 1871 when Wilhelm I of Prussia became the first Kaiser of a united Germany. In one typical article, he promoted the theory that opera (implying his own) had a kinship with the towering pinnacle of human creativity, the ancient

Greek tragedies. It was then only a logical step for Wagner to propose that *'The subject matter of such works, though purely human, would be the deepest things of life. Far from being entertainment, they would be almost religious enactments.'* To achieve this 'religious' atmosphere, the auditorium had to be darkened and the orchestra pit lowered, all of which came about in his own theatre in Bayreuth, paid for largely by his patron, Ludwig II of Bavaria, and by Wagner himself personally canvassing international subscriptions. The seats were, and still are, deliberately uncomfortable so as to focus the audience's attention on the stage rituals. And for the first time in opera the orchestra was totally hidden. His audiences experienced *religious enactments* exactly as he intended, which he now designated as music dramas or *Gesamkunstwerk*. When Wagner's music dramas were performed at Covent Garden towards the end of the century the English audiences were not amused by his insistence on total darkness or his equally irritating non-admittance of latecomers.

Wagner embedded his political and social philosophy in his *Gesamkunstwerk* by impregnating the ancient Nordic myths with intense nationalism coupled with a deep undercurrent of eroticism and rabid anti-Semitism. Hans Sachs, the simple cobbler in *Die Meistersinger* became the patriarch of all German art and artists. At the other end of the spectrum, Alberich in *Das Rhinegold* epitomized the conniving and groveling Jew. His anti-Semitism was so virulent that a pianist, Rubinstein (not the Russian composer) was so ashamed of his Jewish inheritance that he offered himself as a repetiteur without a fee 'to atone for the sins of his race'. However, with his usual myopia, Wagner sacked the pianist because the singers informed him that Rubinstein lacked rhythm, a 'typical Israelite weakness'!

Wagner's *Der Ring des Nibelungen* was composed during the heyday of moral respectability yet Siegmund and Sieglinde had an incestuous relationship which produced a son, Siegfried, who, they prophesied, would grow to manhood to become the saviour of the world! Wagner's own personal life also came up against contemporary mores in that he seduced Cosima, the illegitimate daughter of Franz Liszt and the wife of his ardent disciple Hans von Bülow; inevitably they named the outcome of their illicit union, Siegfried! Yet Cosima could confide in her diaries that the latest fashion of ladies showing their ankles was highly immoral! Social revolutions and historical changes have always influenced the development of music and opera but with Wagner it seems to have been the other way round. His music dramas profoundly affected the young Adolf Hitler to such an extent that the Nazi myth about racial purity grew out of Wagner's theories, and in time was to become the core of their 'philosophy'.

The Italian composers had been following a quite different path arising out of their more 'earthy' personality and a natural propensity for melody. The *Bel Canto* school had come into being with the operas of Bellini, Donizetti and Rossini, with the 'melodramas' *Norma*, *I Puritani*, *Lucia di Lammermoor*, *Anna Bolena*, *Maria Stuarda* and *Guillaume Tell*. All of them are regularly performed today but others such as Bellini's *Il Pirata* and Rossini's *Otello* have been forgotten, the latter probably because it was later overshadowed by Verdi's penultimate masterpiece. Bellini's penchant was for elegiac vocal lines, which greatly influenced Chopin whose piano writing, especially in the Nocturnes, might easily have been written by the Italian composer. Donizetti and Rossini, on the other hand, were equally at home in *opera buffa* with such superb masterpieces as *Don Pasquale*, *L'elisir d'amore*, *La fille du régiment*, *Il barbiere di Siviglia* and *La Cenerentola*.

Verdi inherited their melodic gifts though arguably with an even greater dramatic instinct. He was born in the same year as Wagner (1813), and when he died in 1901, after composing *Otello* and *Falstaff* at the ripe young age of eighty, virtually the whole of Milan lined the streets for his funeral to pay their respects. Like Wagner, Verdi was an ardent patriot and such was the state of affairs in his youth that one singer was nearly imprisoned for having sung the word *libertà* on stage. The subject matter of his early operas also had a profound extra-musical significance on his compatriots especially the chorus of Israelites singing *Va pensiero* in *Nabucco*. The general public were able to call out <u>V</u>iva <u>E</u>mmanuel <u>R</u>e <u>D</u>i <u>I</u>talia as a rallying cry, the initials incidentally spelling out his surname, thus avoiding the censorship. Nevertheless throughout his long life, Verdi kept aloof from active politics.

For the next generation of Italian composers, *verismo* (realism) defined the operas of Mascagni, Leoncavallo and Puccini whose *La bohème* (1896) explored the *exotic* world of the Parisian demi-monde and its poverty stricken artists, the 'Bohemians'. The opera was produced in the same year that Henry Ford invented the motor car, and both have dominated the world ever since. But the real world of the proletariat was portrayed by the French composer Charpentier in his *Louise*. In Russia and Eastern Europe, the rising ferment of nationalism encouraged a repertoire based on their folk tales and epics such as Smetana's *Bartered Bride* and *Dalibor*, Dvořák's *Rusalka* and Borodin's *Prince Igor*. But of the operas by Glinka, Dargomijsky, Rimsky-Korsakov, Borodin and the eleven by Tchaikovsky, only *Eugene Onegin*, *Pikovaya Dama* (The Queen of Spades) and Mussorgsky's *Boris Godunov* have managed to attract an audience in the West.

The French evolved their own genre, *Opéra Comique* – a misunderstood title, as it was not necessarily comic and included dialogue instead of recitative. Nor was it *Opéra bouffe*, which was the French equivalent of Italian *Opera buffa*. *Opera Lyrique* was a category that lay halfway between *Opéra Comique* and *Opera Grande* being shorter than the latter, and with less chorus involvement, fewer sumptuous sets and less sophisticated costumes but sung throughout, unlike *Opéra Comique*. The first *Opéra Comique* was actually by an Italian composer, Pergolesi, whose *La serva padrona* was translated into French. It had originally been used as a Divertisement in an *opera seria* but was so successful that it was taken out of its context and became an *opera buffa* in its own right. It was then taken to France where it became an *opéra comique*. Bizet's

Carmen was originally conceived as an *opéra comique*, but later 'improved' by the addition of orchestral recitatives as was Offenbach's only attempt at a serious opera, *Les Contes d'Hoffmann*.

Richard Strauss, Wagner's operatic heir, scandalized the German respectable bourgeoisie with his outrageously daring *Salome* and *Elektra* at first, but then departed from their dissonance and sensationalism into the world of *Der Rosenkavalier*, which has since become his most popular opera. It was set in the era of Maria Theresa, yet infused with the Viennese waltz modeled on those by Johann Strauss (no relation), the 'Waltz King'. With hindsight, this anachronism in *Der Rosenkavalier* seems to reflect the opulence that overlay the rising political unrest which eventually led to the highly civilized and sophisticated citizens of the Weimar Republic being seduced by Nazism. The waltz was the most popular dance of its day and the Viennese Operetta epitomized the reign of the Emperor Franz Joseph, but it took the determination of Gustav Mahler to include *Die Fledermaus* in the regular repertoire of the Vienna State Opera alongside the more 'serious' offerings. Those who scorn Viennese Operetta as being merely the work of third-rank composers who employed others to orchestrate their music little realize that such composers as Lehar and Kálmán engaged such alter egos like the founder of the system of 'composing with twelve tones', Arnold Schoenberg.

A dichotomy in music began to emerge which was to change the face of art and culture which was indirectly related to the expansion of democratic principles in the western world. Whereas the wealthy (educated) strata of society enjoyed concerts, opera and ballet, the lower, blue-collar workers had their own musical entertainment which they had inherited from the Ballad Operas and the folk music of the past: Italy, its Neapolitan songs (influencing Puccini); France and Germany, their cabaret songs; and England, its music hall and front parlour ballads. In America, Vaudeville – a synonym for music hall — was equally popular as were cowboy ballads of the Wild West. The emancipated slaves also contributed their unique musical idiom and popularized their Spirituals, Blues, Ragtime, Dixie and Jazz. Then in the same year that *Der Rosenkavalier* was first performed, 1911, Irving Berlin's 'Alexander's Ragtime Band' opened up a whole new musical era. The composer was Jewish yet the song radiated the cross-fertilization of American, African and Central European as well as Yiddish cultures, which was truly American. Then when Al Johnson (also Jewish) sang in the first 'talkie', *The Jazz Singer* in 1927, American popular music began to be the lingua franca of the western world. The dichotomy that was appearing unconsciously harked back to the medieval Boethius and Augustine in that the stylistic fingerprints of popular music were related to *Musica mundana* while classical music and opera was more in tune with *musica humana*. A generalization perhaps but body language and rhythm is the basis of all popular music while classical/serious/art music stems from the spirit and the soul.

In 1933, George Gershwin, when defining Jazz wrote, '*It is difficult to determine what enduring values, aesthetically, jazz has contributed, because jazz is a word which has been used for at least five or six different types of music. It is really a conglomeration of many things. It has a little bit of ragtime, the blues, classicism and spirituals. Basically it is a matter of rhythm . . . When jazz is played in another nation, it is called American. When it is played in another country it sounds false. Jazz is the result of the energy stored up in America. It is a very energetic kind of music, noisy, boisterous and even vulgar.*' Since that time, however, the word Jazz implies the complex improvisations of a small ensemble of instrumentalists and 'Blues' singers while Gershwin's 'conglomeration' grew into the music of the dance bands, now called popular music and its more recent spin-off, pop.

George Gershwin started out as a 'song plugger' in Tin Pan Alley, the Mecca of music publishing, and developed into a composer in his own right, but like Offenbach before him, he craved for recognition by his 'classical' colleagues. After composing a number of brilliant musicals and reviews he went on to write *Porgy & Bess*, but it has remained pigeon-holed as both a musical and an opera while its arias (songs) are sung by opera and jazz singers alike. Gershwin had stipulated that it should always be performed by an Afro-American cast and it was half a century before *Porgy & Bess* was presented at one of the pinnacles of 'high art', Glyndebourne. Nevertheless Glyndebourne obeyed Gershwin's stipulation so the chorus was specially recruited from West Indian singers domiciled in England who complemented the Afro-American principals.

In Germany meanwhile, jazz opera was attempted but such works as Ernst Krenek's *Jonny spielt auf* were only marginally successful and are now virtually forgotten. The runaway hit was *Der Dreigroschenoper* by Kurt Weill and Bertolt Brecht, which was a sophisticated version of the cabaret song idiom, as popular in Berlin as had been its model *The Beggars Opera* in London centuries before. With the rise of National Socialism, Kurt Weill went to America but was only moderately successful with the American Musical idiom, though recently there have been revivals of his Broadway shows like *Knickerbocker Holiday*, *Lady in the Dark* and *Lost in the Stars*. Since the Second World War, many European companies now include Musicals (Music Theatre) in their repertoire such as *Oklahoma*, *Kiss me Kate*, *Fiddler on the Roof*, *Show Boat* and *Sweeney Todd*.

Frederick Delius, who rarely expressed his views publicly, is quoted in an interview in 1919 as saying, '*The future of opera generally as an art form? Length and cumbersomeness, in my opinion, will be the first feature to disappear . . . Long dialogues and wearisome narrations must go, and will be replaced by short, strong emotional impressions given in a series of terse scenes. Ninety minutes to two hours is long enough for any opera.* 'His prophecy has not been fulfilled by any means, but opera has now arrived at yet another crisis – not by *long dialogues* or *wearisome narrations* or even singers' vocal excesses – but by the very foundation of opera, its music that now fails to communicate with the general public.

Opera only came into existence three to four hundred years ago and, as in nature, in which everything that is born, dies, it should not be assumed that opera will exist in the future, at least in its present form. In this context, it should be remembered that Middle English, Chaucer and Shakespeare are already becoming unintelligible even with extensive footnotes and will soon die or be 'translated', as if from a foreign language. To recapitulate on opera's phoenix-like ability, Mozart's *Don Giovanni*, subtitled *dramma giocosa* (jocular, humorous) and his *singspiel, Die Zauberflöte*, a play with music – despite its Masonic implications – were still *entertainments*. Then, when the Romantic movement came into being in the nineteenth century, opera became an 'Art' along with painting and sculpture, and this concept, with its superlative High Art, lasted well into the twentieth century.

Today everything is in flux. 'Art' is used indiscriminately to denote anything from 'state of the art' car manufacture to sport and pop music, whether performed with or without any expertise. It is now virtually impossible to define what Art really is. Like 'culture' and 'heritage', art has become a synonym for any marketable entertainment. Another cliché, 'elitist', is used to denigrate those who enjoy what 'art' previously meant even though the dictionary defines elite as *'the choice or best part'*. The denigration is based to a certain extent on envy for everyone is – or should be – elitist in his or her own particular sphere; a similar attitude is voiced in China about its highly sophisticated Opera.

Opera in the West is stigmatized as the plaything of the idle rich – but even if that sweeping statement is true, their patronage subsidizes opera for those with genuine interest yet who lack the financial wherewithal. Various attempts have been made to woo larger audiences from the 'blue-collar' strata of society but it is not simply a matter of affording the price of a ticket, for as much if not more is spent each year attending sports events. It is rather a question of atti-tude and education – in the best sense of the word – for opera requires both a general and a musical education that supports an innate sensi-bility. If education in 'classical' music and opera was comprehensively introduced, as has been happening in sport and athletics, the situation would be alleviated. Hence it is encouraging to discover that some opera companies have already established out-reach programmes of this kind.

A significant part of the ignorance surrounding opera is that the general public are only aware of 'classical' versus popular music with the latter having subdivisions; pop (as distinct from popular), hard rock, soul, blues, rap, jazz, rock, folk, country and western, world music and contemporary – implying that no contemporary 'classical' composers exist! Genuine folk (including country) music were once the life blood of society but there is now no real equivalent as folk music is no longer anonymous but written by pop singers in an ersatz idiom. In the early 1960s, the recording studios encouraged and promoted the birth of pop groups, basically consisting of electric guitars and drum kits; long spanned melodies disappeared, concentra-tion spans shortened, and a very basic vocabulary was the norm.

Popular music, on the other hand, developed from the dance music of the Big Band era, Musicals and the American Music Theatre – with fascinating harmonies, formal construction and long spanned phrases For the vast majority of today's affluent society, popular music expresses their deepest emotions as witnessed at Princess Diana's funeral, the Memorial Service for the victims of terrorism in Bali, and other examples of public grief. Popular music finally became respectable when it received the accolade of Queen Elizabeth's Jubilee celebration, yet her predecessors would have commissioned Handel, Sullivan, Elgar, Walton or other 'classical' composers to write appropriate music for the occasion. In the year 2002, this was not considered the right path to follow even though a Last Night at the Proms did take place in the gardens of Buckingham Palace – perhaps to placate the diehards! The opera-going public is therefore having to accept the fact that 'popular' music is now as emotionally fulfilling for the vast majority of people as Mozart, Beethoven, Verdi or Puccini is for them.

Social and artistic relevance has been seriously affected by the advent of postmodernism in opera and has alienated some of the traditional audience without necessarily attracting a new public. Paradoxically, while authenticity is sought in musical interpretation, postmodern productions are becoming more and more bizarre and show scant respect for their original creators. On the other hand, the seventeenth-century portrait painters clothed their biblical characters in contemporary dress and Shakespeare took many older plots and 'updated' them. But there is a marked difference between a creator who deliberately sets his work in a contemporary period well before putting pen to paper, and the postmodern re-creator who then disfigures the original conception. Verdi actually set *La traviata* in his own time but its relevance was unacceptable to his first audience, which he had to admit in a letter to a friend: *'Other composers would not have written it because of the conventions, the epoch and many other scruples'*. Nearly a century later, Richard Strauss felt the need to write, *'The worst thing of all is if in* Die Zauberflöte *the sets are made to clash stylistically with the work especially by the use of lavishly modernized décor, properly speaking, it should involve rewriting the libretto in the "modern style" and re-orchestrating in the style of Götterdämmerung.'* If he were alive to day, Strauss might have suggested (with typical ironic humour), that *Die Zauberflöte* should be performed by a pop group!

The other negative affect of postmodernism is that the audience's attention is diverted from the interplay of musical and dramatic characters to the fantastic stage settings and technology. The result is that when a postmodern *Rigoletto* is performed, it takes on the aura of a twentieth-century Italian movie with Verdi transformed into a nineteenth-century counterpart of a film composer. This should not imply that new productions of the standard repertoire must only be fossilized museum pieces as there are many stimulating new realizations. One such brilliant realization was a semi-staged concert performance of *Die Zauberflöte* with the orchestra and singers on stage together. Papageno's traditional pipes were discarded, and instead he whistled the famous five notes as he ran his fingers across his lips. The 'sets' were provided entirely by dancers who were grouped differently for each scene to become in turn the dragon, the temple portals, the wild animals and the Queen of the Night's chariot. The performance even had interplay between Papageno and the conductor, yet throughout there was not a trace of anachronistic technology.

Any new production, whether postmodern or not, depends on the quality of its presentation and going hand-in-hand with the music to enthrall the audience. During the eighteenth century audiences always craved for the new rather than looking back to the old, as did audiences in the late nineteenth and early twentieth centuries, so it is now only right and proper that opera springs from its own ethos. Technology is not necessarily the answer, for though videos and DVDs with the world's finest singers and orchestras are now readily available, it creates its own problems. Superb video recordings may squeeze many of the less affluent opera companies out of existence and erode the grass-roots experience from which new generations of performers develop, and in turn affect the progression of artists from that level all the way up to those companies that produce the video recordings. Another important factor, at the moment hardly considered, is that the Western world is experiencing a great influx of many people and cultures from the Middle East, India and Asia. Perhaps alongside their traditional forms of expression and entertainment, classical music and opera will take their place – at least by the second and third generation. One sincerely hopes so, for this will inevitably have a great influence on the future creation and enjoyment of opera.

In a recent television interview, Pierre Boulez summed up the situation facing arts and artists now and in the future, *'We must be aware of the past without being a prisoner of the past'*. Following that succinct advice, it is now time to abandon the idea that opera is moribund to search for new styles of composition and new ways to perform. Both creators and re-creators need to be supreme educators. They need to improve their powers of communication or Western civilization may return to the Dark Ages. However, opera always has been, and should always be, *exotic* and *irrational* regardless of genre, medium or style. For the quotation from Dr. Johnson with which this book began actually provides us with significant hope. Opera is *'an exotic and irrational entertainment which has always been combated, and always has prevailed.'*

Glossary

Accompagnato	A recitative accompanied by instrumental ensemble rather than a continuo instrument.
A piacere	To be performed as the performer 'pleases' implying a certain freedom.
Appoggiatura	'Leaning' from one note to another, i.e. passing through.
Aria	An air or song in an opera or oratorio.
Arietta	A shorter and/or lighter vocal solo than an aria.
Arioso	A phrase in a recitative to be sung more than 'spoken' (parlando).
Ausgabe	German, literally meaning 'giving out' but has come to mean an edition.
Ballad Opera	A seventeenth and early eighteenth-century English Entertainment using the popular songs of the day but with satirical texts.
Balance	Equality between voice and orchestra. Conductors are often criticized for allowing the orchestra to play too loudly and overbalancing the singers, but this is often due to the singer's lack of projection.
Barcarolle	Venetian Gondolier's song in 6/8 time suggested by the rhythm of waves lapping against the Gondola. Verdi's *Otello* and Offenbach's *Les Contes d'Hoffmann* include Barcarolles.
Baroque	Originally an architectural term meaning excessively ornate or extravagant.
Bel canto	Italian for beautiful singing but it also refers to the florid vocal style of nineteenth-century Italian opera.
Bocca chiusa	Italian for closed mouth (*Bouche fermée* in French). The off-stage chorus in *Madama Butterfly* is requested to sing *bocca chiusa*, i.e. hum.
Brindisi	An Italian drinking song having presumably originated in the city of Brindisi. Examples are in Verdi's *La traviata* and *Macbeth*.

Brio	With vigour or spirit.
Cabaletta	Has various meanings; a short aria, an aria in rondo form or the final florid section of an aria or duet.
Cadence	The Latin 'to fall', which came to mean the conclusion of a musical phrase.
Cadenza	Italian for cadence when the performer has an opportunity to exhibit his or her technical prowess; usually at the end of an aria but sometimes in the middle.
Canon (*or Round*)	Singing a canon was a popular pastime in which any number of singers would join in the ensemble, repeating the same phrase at specified moments. Operatic canons occur in the Finale of Mozart's *Così fan tutte* and Britten's *Peter Grimes*.
Cantabile	Implying an extra singing and smooth quality.
Cantilena	Diminutive for 'little song' meaning a legato phrase without florid decoration.
Canzone	Italian (diminution, canzonetta) for a simple aria in a flowing style. Originally from Naples where it had been a popular song in dialect and in 6/8 time. Mozart used the title several times but without Neapolitan connotations.
Castrato	A male singer who underwent a surgical operation before puberty to preserve the soprano quality of his voice. The last public performance was in 1844 but one castrato has been preserved on a very early recording.
Cavatina	A short aria in one section. Yet Figaro's cavatina *'se vuol ballare'* in Mozart's opera is in three sections, the third part being a reprise of the first.
Cembalo	The Italian equivalent of the German Clavier or Klavier; usually the harpsichord that filled out the figured bass of a continuo part.
Chaconne	A synonym for Passacaglia or Ground Bass in which the bass line is continuously repeated while variations occur above. Originally a slow dance based on a three-bar phrase. Operatic examples include Dido's Lament in Purcell's *Dido & Aeneas* and Britten's *Peter Grimes, Albert Herring* and *Death in Venice*.
Chromatic	Non diatonic notes adding colour to the diatonic scale.
Claque	Members of the audience paid by the artist or an impresario to lead the applause.

Clavier	The name for a keyboard instrument used for *secco recitative* in opera. Alternative names include Klavier (the German equivalent) and Cembalo.
Colla Voce	Italian for 'with the voice part' implying freedom of tempo for the singer. A synonym for *a piacere*.
Coloratura	Italian for 'coloured' implying highly florid and brilliant vocal writing.
Continuo	Used to indicate the harpsichord recitatives that fill out the harmonies from the figured bass, but may mean any plucked instrument fulfilling the same purpose. In *Opera seria* the continuo consisted of a double-bass and a cello but in *Opera buffa* it was only played by the cello without double bass, allowing for greater vivacity.
Contra Dance	A country dance usually in quick 3/8 time.
Cuts	Until the twentieth century composers wrote alternate passages to allow for the singers to make cuts as they wished. *'An opera is known by its cuts'*, says Monsieur Jordan in Moliere's *Le bourgeois Gentilhomme* in Hofmannsthal's version for Richard Strauss.
Da Capo	Italian for 'from the head' meaning to return to the beginning after the middle section in a contrasting mood and/or key. The reprise was usually ornamented.
Deus ex machina	At the height of a plot's complexity the hand of God is suddenly revealed to unravel the knot.
Diatonic	The eight notes of a key; the intervals being tone, tone, semi-tone, tone, tone, semi-tone.
Dirigent	German for Conductor.
Dolce	Italian for 'with sweetness'.
Dramaturg	The person responsible for all literary aspects of the libretto, progamme notes and background of the opera.
Duet	For two voices in any combination, i.e. two Sopranos, Tenor and Bass, Baritone and Mezzo, etc.
Duettino	Diminutive of duet implying a lighter or more playful version.
Durchkomponiert	German for 'through composed'. It originally meant a lied in which the music was different for each stanza. During the nineteenth century, it came to be used to describe continuous music for the orchestra without any harpsichord recitatives.

Embellishment	The decoration of the vocal line with mordents, trills, appoggiaturas and other ornamentation.
Ensemble	Any number of performers, either vocal or instrumental or both.
Erste Kapellmeister	The 'first conductor', meaning a subordinate to the Musical Director in a German opera house.
Fach	German for vocal categories.
Falsetto	Literally meaning false and therefore unnatural for the male voice.
Fandango	An eighteenth-century Spanish dance accompanied by guitars and castanets in a brisk triple time tempo. Gluck's *Don Juan* has a fandango which Mozart 'borrowed' for Act 3 of *Le nozze di Figaro* although it is more like a minuet.
Figured Bass	The harmonic structure expressed in numerical shorthand under the bass line of the continuo part.
Fioritura	Italian for 'flowering' originally meaning the decoration extemporized by the singer; now a general term for florid music.
Flats	The moveable parts of the stage set.
From the top	The modern colloquialism for *da capo* meaning 'from the beginning'.
Fugue	A contrapuntal form in any number of parts using a single theme that enters at various degrees of the scale and at different moments. Operatic fugues are rare but they include the Finale of Verdi's *Falstaff* and the Fire & Water scene in Mozart's *Die Zauberflöte* (juxtaposed with a North German Protestant Chorale!)
Fugato	Fugal writing in a non-fugal composition and not strictly following the rules of fugue. Examples include the Overture to Mozart's *Die Zauberflöte* and the Act I Finale of his *Così fan tutte*.
Gavotte	A dance of French origin in a steady 2/2 tempo beginning on the second beat of the bar. An operatic example is the famous Gavotte in Massenet's *Manon*.
Grand Opera	Originally the English term for a serious opera wihout dialogue. In France it implied an opera involving spectacular or historical subjects. They had large casts and a ballet and

were usually in five acts.Today the term is haphazardly used to mean any opera regardless of genre.

Ground Bass	See Chaconne.
Habanera	Originally a Cuban dance from Havana with two slow beats to the bar. It became very popular in Spain and with French composers. Carmen sings and dances the most famous operatic Habanera.
Head voice	The upper register of a voice. It is experienced in the head, although more of a psychological than physiological sensation.
In scena	Italian for a production rehearsal usually with the sets and costumes.
Instrumental obligato	See Obligato.
Interlude	Orchestral music played while the sets are being changed between scenes. Debussy's *Pelléas et Mélisande* and a number of Britten's operas include Interludes.
Intermezzo	Italian for 'in the middle', a synonym for Interlude.
Klavier	See Clavier or Cembalo above.
Köchel, Ludwig von (1800–1877)	A botanist and minerologist who first catalogued all of Mozart's works. His name is usually abbreviated to 'K' in the scores.
Ländler	A German forerunner of the slightly slower Austrian Waltz .
Libretto	Italian for 'littlebook', meaning the text of an opera.
Leitmotiv	German for 'a leading motive'; a short musical figure or theme to represent a character or mood. Wagner used these pithy melodic and/or rhythmic cells to ceate a symphonic texture for the orchestra but he never referred to them as Leitmotiv preferring to use the terms Hauptmotive, Thematisches Motiv and Grundthema.
Lyric Opera	An opera of a more intimate nature than Grand Opera.
Maestro	Italian for 'Master' meaning a teacher. In church music he was the Maestro di Capella and in Germany, Kapellmeister. Italian conductors are called maestro as a sign of respect but it has come to be used internationally even when not warranted.
Marcia	Italian for a march or procession.
Masking	The term for whatever or whoever may be blocking the singer's view on stage.

Masque	An English sixteenth- and seventeenth-century term for court entertainments involving speech and song, although the plot was conveyed in the dance. The principal characters were called masquers.
Melodrama	The original Italian name for opera as being a drama with melody but it has come to mean any over-exaggerated drama or false histrionics.
Melos	The Greek word for melody. Now implying the inner unheard line that runs through a phrase or movement.
Menuetto or Minuetto	An Italian dance (Minuet in English; Menuett in German) in 3/4 time.
Mezza voce	Italian for middle of the voice and not a dynamic marking as is sometimes believed.
Music Theatre	(a) contemporary avante garde opera; (b) a recently acquired name for the American Musical.
Obligato	Italian for obligatory, meaning that during arias or vocal ensembles an instrumentalist is 'obliged' to play the solos.
O.P.	The opposite side of the stage to the prompt corner. It is sometimes reversed depending on the structure of the building.
Opera Buffa	Italian (French, Opéra Bouffe) originally meaning a comic opera with characters from the lower end of the social spectrum and was performed as comic relief in the middle of an opera seria.
Opéra Comique	A French term first used in 1715 to describe a parody of Grand Opera. It had spoken drama rather than sung recitatives between the arias and was not necessarily comic but an opera with comedy.
Opera Seria	Italian for 'Serious opera' on mythological or aristocratic subjects with little action and with the drama conveyed principally by its vocal interpretation.
Operetta	Diminutive of opera implying more entertaining and lighter subjects than in opera.
Overture	The orchestral movement played before the rise of the curtain as an introduction and to quieten the audience. In recent times, producers have used overtures as an integral part of the production. Some composers like Puccini and Britten have dispensed with overtures altogether.

Pants roles	A modern colloquialism for Travesty roles (q.v.).
Parlando	Italian for 'speaking'. Although parlando passages are sung on pitch, the intention '*parlando*' is to give an impression of speech.
Partitur	German for an orchestral score.
Passagio	Italian for 'passage' meaning the bridge between the singer's middle and upper registers.
Passacaglia	See Chaconne.
Patter Song	A comic song revelling in speed of performance The most well-known occur in Gilbert & Sullivan. Dr. Bartolo's aria in Mozart's *Le nozze di Figaro* and Rossini's *Largo al factotum* were forerunners.
Perruquiere	The male member of the technical staff responsible for maintaining wigs and grooming hair.
Perruquière	The female equivalent.
Play out	A modern colloquialism for postlude.
Portamento	Italian to 'carry' the voice from one note to another usually over a wide interval. No to be confused with 'glissando' meaning to 'slide'.
Postlude	The orchestral music after the voice has finished. The modern colloquialism is 'play out'.
Postmodern	A production set in the twentieth century but for an opera of a previous era with anachronsims such as cars and helicopters.
Prelude	A short overture such as Verdi's *Macbeth* or Tchaikovsky's *Eugene Onegin*.
Projection	Based on the *Bel Canto* technique to carry the voice into the auditorium.
Proscenium Arch	The structure that frames the stage.
Recitativo secco	Italian for 'dry recitative' with harpsichord accompaniment rather than orchestral. The continuo player was expected to extemporize on the figured bass with a musical commentary on the drama.
Recitative accompanimento	Italian for recitative with orchestral accompaniment.
Ritornello	Italian for 'a little return' meaning the orchestral passage before or after the soloist in an aria or concerto.
Rondo	An aria in which the principal theme returns a number of times

	as in the Finale of Rossini's *La Cenerentola* and Mozart's instrumental concertos.
Rubato	Italian 'to rob' the time but the performer must repay the 'borrowed' time within the phrase or it becomes a rallentando (slowing down). A rubato allows for romantic expression within the overall pulse.
Seguidilla	A Castilian folk song and dance in a quick 3/4 or 3/8 time. The most famous operatic seguidilla occurs in Bizet's *Carmen*.
Sicilienne	A baroque dance in 6/8 time. Originally a Sicilian pagan fertility rite.
Sinfonia	The synonym for Preludio or Prelude.
Singspiel	A German entertainment with spoken dialogue and music.
Sipario	Italian for the stage curtain.
Sitzprobe	The German for an orchestral rehearsal in which the singers sit and concentrate on the orchestra and not the production.
Sostitutto	Italian for understudy.
Sotto voce	Italian for 'under the voice'. It is not a synonym for *pp* but a quasi whisper of a special character for dramatic atmosphere. It occurs frequently in Mozart's operas and orchestral works.
Souffleur	The French word for the prompter.
Stage Director	A synonym for Producer.
Stagione	Italian for 'seasonal' implying a resident company performing in short seasons often with guest artists.
Stretto Finale	Italian for a Finale in which the momentum increases scene by scene to heighten the drama, the audience's enthusiasm and to encourage applause. Mozart's stretto finale (*Figaro*, Act 2) is a classic example and Rossini exploited the form in his comic operas.
Surtitles	A recent invention providing translations of foreign texts above the proscenium arch. It tends to lessen the audience's concentration on the stage but is very useful for those who do not understand the original language.
Terzetto	Italian diminutive of Trio.
Tessitura	Italian for the various vocal ranges.
Travesty Role	A rôle sung by the voice of the opposite sex literally translated today as 'pants role'. Known in Germany as Hosenrole. Cherubino, Sesto, Octavian, Orpheus and many other rôles are

in this fach. Cherubino is an adolescent boy about to enter puberty so that the female voice in a male costume admirably expresses his sexual ambiguity. In the seventeenth century, rôles were often interchanged between the genders and Johann Adolf Hasse composed the rôle of Cleopatra for Farinelli and Mark Antony for Vittoria Tesi. By the eighteenth century only the female voice in the male costume remained.

Trio	For three performers in any combination of parts.
Tutti	Italian for an ensemble involving all the performers.
Upstage / *Downstage*	Upstage is the area furthest from the audience, and downstage the area nearest to the audience
Ur-text	German for the original score or text.
Vaudeville	In Ballad Operas and Singspiels the Vaudeville concluded the entertainment with the singers bidding adieu to the audience.
Verismo	The name for Italian operas around the beginning of the twentieth century based on very dramatic texts about the lower strata of society, as in Mascagni's *Cavalleria Rusticana*.
Vibrato	Used on stringed instruments to add warmth to the tone, but with singers it can develop into a wobble and becomes decidedly unpleasant.
Vocal Coach	A specialist in coaching rôles but not a singing teacher.
Vocal Score	A reduction of the full orchestral score to be played on the piano. It is used by conductors, repetiteurs and singers for study and rehearsal purposes.
Voix Blanche	A French term translated as 'white voice', i.e. without vibrato. It was extensively used at one time for 'mad' rôles such as Lucia di Lammermoor but it has almost dropped out of fashion.
Vorspiel	The German for Prelude.
Waltz	A Viennese dance in 3/4 time (see Ländler) with a basic one harmony per bar. It grew to popularity in the nineteenth century.

Source of Quotations

Accoustics   PAGE 15   *This Festival Opera House . . .*
John Christie. Glyndebourne Festival Programme, 1934.

Applause   PAGE 94   *A great deal of noise . . .*
Mozart: The man and the artist. Compiled and annotated by Friedrich Kerst; translated and edited by Henry Krehbiel. Dover Publications, New York, 1965.

Baton   PAGE 75   *I produced my baton . . .*
Louis Spohr. *Musicians on Musicians,* edited by. F. Bonavia. Routledge & Kegan Paul Ltd., 1956.

Composing for the theatre   PAGE 7   *You can feel . . .*
The Complete Operas of Mozart, by Charles Osborne. Da Capo Press, 1978.

PAGE 15   *Our music differs . . .*
Verdi. *Composers on Music,* edited by Sam Morgenstern. Bonanza Books. Copyright MCMLVI Pantheon Books Inc.

PAGE 15   *I have the great weakness . . .*
Puccini. *Composers on Music,* edited by Sam Morgenstern. Bonanza Books. Copyright MCMLVI Pantheon Books Inc.

The Conductor   PAGE 28   *definition of a conductor . . .*
An article in *Musical Opinion,* London, 1890.

Health   PAGE 45   *The results may not be applicable . . .*
A. W. Sedgwick. Institute for Fitness & Research and Training Inc. North Adelaide, South Australia, 1987.

Irrationality   PAGE 15   *The irrationality of opera . . .*
Bertolt Brecht, trans. J. Willett. *The Faber Book of Opera,* Tom Sutcliffe. Faber & Faber, 2000.

Keys   PAGE 10   *One cites the sharp . . .*
Rita Steblin, *A History of Key Characteristics in the Early Eighteenth and Nineteenth Centuries.* UMI Research Press.

Opera   PAGE 3   *I have thought it necessary . . .*
The Wordsworth Dictionary of Musical Quotations, by Derek Watson. Wordsworth, 1994.
PAGE 3   *Musik and Poetry, have been . . .*
Composers on Music, edited by Sam Morgenstern. Bonanza Books. Copyright MCMLVI Pantheon Books Inc.
PAGE 124   *The worst thing of all . . .*
Richard Strauss, *Betrachtungen und Erinnerungen*, trans. Boosey & Hawkes. Zurich, Atlantis, 1949.

Orchestra   PAGE 9   *I have noticed . . .*
Monteverdi, trans. D. Stevens. *The Faber Book of Opera*, Tom Sutcliffe. Faber & Faber, 2000.
PAGE 51   *And yet this malicious mob . . .*
Richard Strauss, *Betrachtungen und Erinnerungen*, trans. Boosey & Hawkes. Zurich, Atlantis, 1949.

Overtures   PAGE 18   *The best time to . . .*
G. Mazzatinti and F. G. Manis, editors, *Lettere di G. Rossini*. Florence, Barbera, 1902/ *Composers on Music*, edited by Sam Morgenstern. Bonanza Books. Copyright MCMLVI Pantheon Books Inc.

Promotion   PAGE 89   *Why not come and live . . .*
John Christie. Glyndebourne Festival Programme, 1934.

Singers   PAGE 55   *How wonderful . . .*
The Wordsworth Dictionary of Musical Quotations, by Derek Watson. Wordsworth, 1994.
PAGE 55   *Germany has no lack . . .*
Interviews and Encounters with Verdi, edited and annotated by Marcello Conati, trans. Richard Stokes. Victor Gollancz, 1984.

Tempo   PAGE 10   *All the best philosophers . . .*
The Pleasures of Music, edited by Jaques Barzun. University of Chicago Press, 1951/1977.

Libretto   PAGE 21   *On the stage . . .*
The Wordsworth Dictionary of Musical Quotations, by Derek Watson. Wordsworth, 1994.
PAGE 21   *A writer of an operatic libretto . . .*
From *Il teatro alla monda*, 1720. Benedetto Marcello, trans.

	Richard G. Pauly. *The Musical Quarterly*. New York, July 1948/*Composers on Music*, edited by Sam Morgenstern. Bonanza Books. Copyright MCMLVI Pantheon Books Inc.
The audience	PAGE 90 *The average man of the present day . . .* Delius. First published in *The Sackbut*, editor Philip Heseltine. J. Curwen & Sons, 1920/*Composers on Music*, edited by Sam Morgenstern. Bonanza Books. Copyright MCMLVI Pantheon Books Inc.
The future	PAGE 121 *The future of opera . . .* Delius. First published in *The Sackbut*, editor Philip Heseltine. J. Curwen & Sons, 1920/*Composers on Music*, edited by Sam Morgenstern. Bonanza Books. Copyright MCMLVI Pantheon Books Inc.
Jazz opera	PAGE 120 *It is difficult to determine . . .* George Gershwin. *Composers on Music*, edited by Sam Morgenstern. Bonanza Books. Copyright MCMLVI Pantheon Books Inc.

Bibliography

Berlioz, Hector. *Les Soirèes de l'orchestre*. Translated by C. R. Fortescue with an Introduction and notes by David Cairns. Penguin Books, 1963.

Berlioz/Strauss. *Grand traité d'instrumentation et d'orchestration modernes*. Translated by Theodore Font. Dover edition, 1991.

Bing, Sir Rudolf. *A Knight at the Opera*. G. P. Putnam's Sons, New York, 1981.

Cooke, Deryck. *The Language of Music*. Oxford University Press, 1959.

Da Ponte, Lorenzo. *Memoirs*. Translated by Elisabeth Abbott. Dover, 1967.

Dent, Edward J. *Opera*. Pelican Books, 1945.

Falkner, Sir Keith. *Voice/Yehudi Menuhin Music Guides*. Macdonald & Co., London and Sydney, 1983.

Fredman, Myer. *The Conductor's Domain: A guide for aspiring maestri*. Thames Publishing/Elkin Music Services, 2001.

Fredman, Myer. *From* Idomeneo *to* Die Zauberflöte*: A conductor's commentary*. Sussex Academic Press, Brighton and Portland, 2002.

Magee, Brian. *Aspects of Wagner*. Panther Books, 1978.

Macdonald, Patrick. *The Alexander Technique AS I SEE IT*. The Alpha Press/Sussex Academic Press, Brighton and Portland, 2002.

Morgenstern, Sam. *Composers on Music*. Bonanza Books, 1996.

Sutcliffe, Tom. *The Faber Book of Opera*. Faber & Faber, 2000.

Strauss, Richard. *Betrachtungen und Erinnerungen*. Atlantis, Zurich, 1949. English translation, *Recollections & Reflections*. Boosey & Hawkes.

Strauss/Hofmannsthal. *A Working Friendship*. Translated by Hanns Hammelmann and Ewald Osers. Vienna House, 1974.

Wagner, Cosima. *Diaries* (2 volumes). Translated by Geoffrey Skelton. Collins, 1978.

Walter, Bruno. *Of Music and Music Making*. Translated by Paul Hamburger. W.W. Norton & Co. Inc, 1957. English translation copyright 1961, Faber & Faber Ltd.

Watson, Derek. *The Worsworth Dictionary of Musical Quotations*. Wordsworth Edition, 1994.

Index

Index

Papageno.